World Wisdom
The Library of Perennial Philosophy

The Library of Perennial Philosophy is dedicated to the exposition of the timeless Truth underlying the diverse religions. This Truth, often referred to as the *Sophia Perennis*—or Perennial Wisdom—finds its expression in the revealed Scriptures as well as in the writings of the great sages and the artistic creations of the traditional worlds.

Songs without Names: Volumes VII-XII appears as one of our selections in the Writings of Frithjof Schuon series.

The Writings of Frithjof Schuon

The Writings of Frithjof Schuon form the foundation of our library because he is the preeminent exponent of the Perennial Philosophy. His work illuminates this perspective in both an essential and comprehensive manner like none other.

Songs without Names

Volumes VII-XII

Poems by

Frithjof Schuon

Foreword by

Annemarie Schimmel

Introduction by

William Stoddart

Translated from the German

World Wisdom

Library of Congress Cataloging-in-Publication Data

Schuon, Frithjof, 1907-1998.
[Poems. English. Selections]
Songs without names, VII-XII : poems / by Frithjof Schuon ; foreword by Annemarie Schimmel ; introduction by William Stoddart.
p. cm. — (Writings of Frithjof Schuon) (The library of perennial philosophy)
"Translated from the German."
Includes index.
ISBN-13: 978-1-933316-24-6 (pbk. : alk. paper)
ISBN-10: 1-933316-24-1 (pbk. : alk. paper) 1. Schuon, Frithjof, 1907-1998—Translations into English. 2. Religious poetry, German—20th century. I. Schimmel, Annemarie. II. Stoddart, William. III. Title. IV. Series. V. Series: Schuon, Frithjof, 1907-1998. Works. English. 2002.
PT2680.U474A2 2006b
831'.914--dc22

2006016203

Cover: Frithjof Schuon
Photo by Sharlyn Romaine

Printed on acid-free paper in Canada

For information address World Wisdom, Inc.
P.O. Box 2682, Bloomington, Indiana 47402-2682

www.worldwisdom.com

Contents

Foreword

It seems that mystical experience almost inevitably leads to poetry. The great mystics all over the world used the language of poetry when trying to beckon to a mystery that lies beyond normal human experience, and the most glorious works in Eastern and Western religions are the hymns of the mystics, be they Sufis or Christians, Hindus or Zen monks. Different as their expressions are, one feels that the poetical word can more easily lead to the mystery that is hidden behind the veils of intellectual knowledge and which cannot be fettered in logical speech.

In the world of Islam, the love-intoxicated poems of Maulana Jalaladdin Rumi are considered by many to be "the Koran in the Persian tongue," and Rumi is only one of many intoxicated souls who expressed their love and longing, and their experience of the Divine Unity, in verse. And even those mystics who preferred a more "intellectual" approach to the Absolute couched their experiences in verse. The prime example is, of course, Ibn Arabi whose *Tarjuman al-ashwaq* translated his experience of the One, Unattainable Deity into the language of traditional Arabic poetry.

Taking this fact into consideration we are not surprised that Frithjof Schuon too felt compelled to write poetry—and, it is important to note, poetry in his German mother tongue. His verse sometimes reflects ideas and images of R. M. Rilke's *Stundenbuch*, in which the expert on mysticism can find some strange echoes of Ibn Arabi's ideas. This may be an accident, for mystical ideas are similar all over the world; but the German reader of Schuon's verses enjoys the familiar sound. This sound could not be maintained in the English translations of his poetry. Yet, as he himself explains, what really matters is the content, and here we listen to the thinker who, far from the intricate and complex scholarly sentences of his learned prose works, sings the simple prayers of the longing soul: God is the center, the primordial ground which comprehends everything, manifesting Himself through the colorful play of His creations. And it is the human heart which alone can reflect the incomprehensible Being, for humanity's central quality is divinely inspired love, which is the axis of our life.

I hope that Schuon's mystical verse will be read not only by English speaking readers but even more by those who understand German.[1] They will enjoy many of these tender lyrics which show the famous thinker in a very different light and from an unexpected side.

—Annemarie Schimmel, Professor Emeritus, Harvard University

[1] See Translator's Note on page *xvi*

Introduction

Frithjof Schuon (1907-1998) was a sage, an artist, and a poet. During the last three years of his life, he wrote in German—his mother tongue—approximately 3,500 short poems, in 23 separate collections. In content, Schuon's German poems are similar to those in his English collection *Road to the Heart*, but they are much more numerous, and the imagery is even more rich and powerful. The poems cover every possible aspect of metaphysical doctrine, spiritual method, spiritual virtue, and the role and function of beauty. They express every conceivable subtlety of spiritual and moral counsel—and this not merely in general terms, but with uncanny intimacy, detail, and precision. They exhibit incredible sharpness, profundity, comprehensiveness, and compassion. They are his final gift to the world, his testament and his legacy.

Some of the poems are autobiographical, with reminiscences of places experienced: Basle and Paris, the fairy-tale streets of old German towns, Morocco and Andalusia, Turkey and Greece, the American West. Others evoke the genius of certain peoples, such as the Hindus, the Japanese, the Arabs, the Red Indians, and also the Cossacks and the Gypsies. Yet other poems elucidate the role of music, dance, and poetry itself. In one or two poems, the godless modern world comes in for biting, and sometimes fiercely humorous, comment:

Ein weltlich Fest: Lampenkristalle schimmern
Im großen Saal —
Und glänzende Gesellschaft, Damen, Herrn,
Sitzen beim Mahl.
Man spricht von allem und man spricht von nichts —
Der Wein ist rot,
Und so der Blumenschmuck.
Doch keiner, keiner
Denkt an den Tod.

A worldly banquet: chandeliers glitter
In the large hall —
And brilliant society, ladies and gentlemen

Sit down for the meal.
They talk of everything and they talk of nothing –
The wine is red,
And so are the flowers.
But no one, no one
Thinks of death.

(*Stella Maris*, "The Celebration")

The poems embody both severity and compassion. They are powerfully interiorizing. Their content epitomizes Schuon's teaching, which he himself has summarized in the words Truth, Prayer, Virtue, and Beauty. For him, these are the four things needful; they are the very purpose of life, the only source of happiness, and the essential means of salvation. The poems convey these elements to the reader not only mentally, but also, as it were, existentially; their role is both doctrinal and sacramental.

The central role of prayer is powerfully expressed in the following poem entitled "*Panakeia*" ("panacea," the remedy for all ills):

Warum hat Gott die Sprache uns geschenkt?
Für das Gebet.
Weil Gottes Segen dem, der Ihm vertraut,
Ins Herze geht.

Ein Beten ist der allererste Schrei
in diesem Leben.
So ist der letzte Hauch ein Hoffnungswort —
Von Gott gegeben.

Was ist der Stoff, aus dem der Mensch gemacht,
Sein tiefstes Ich?
Es ist das Wort, das uns das Heil gewährt:
Herr, höre mich!

Why has God given us the gift of speech?
For prayer.
Because God's blessing enters the heart of him
Who trusts in God.

The very first cry in this life
Is a prayer.

And the last breath is a word of hope —
Given by God.

What is the substance of which man is made,
His deepest I?
It is the Word that grants us salvation:
Lord, hear me!

(*Stella Maris*, "Panacea")

Many of the poems express the purpose of life with unmistakable clarity, for example:

Jedes Geschöpf ist da, um "Gott" zu sagen;
So musst auch du der Welt Berufung tragen,
O Mensch, der du der Erde König bist —
Weh dem, der seines Daseins Kern vergisst;

Dies tut nicht Tier noch Pflanze, ja kein Stein;
Dies tut der willensfreie Mensch allein
In seinem Wahn.
Sprich "Gott" in deinem Wandern;
Es werde eine Gnade für die Andern.

Denn eine Aura strahlt vom Höchsten Namen —
Gebet ist Segen, ist der Gottheit Samen.

All creatures exist in order to say "God";
So must thou too accept the world's vocation,
O man, who art king of the earth —
Woe unto him who forgets the kernel of his existence;

No animal, no plant nor stone does this;
But only man, with his free will,
In his madness.
Say "God" throughout thy life;
It will be a grace for others too.

For an aura radiates from the Supreme Name —
Prayer is blessing; it is the seed of the Divine.

(*Stella Maris*, "The Aura")

But the dread consequences of a wrong choice are not forgotten:

In Indien sagt man oft, dass Japa-Yoga
Stets Segen bringe — dass das Rāma-Mantra
Ein Wundermittel sei, das helfen müsse.
Dem ist nicht so, denn zürnen kann Shrī Rāma.

In India it is often said that *Japa-Yoga*
Always brings blessings – that the *Rāma-Mantra*
Is a miraculous means, that cannot but help.
This is not so, for Shrī Rāma can also show His wrath.

(*Songs without Names I*-XXXIII)

Und Gottes Zorn — er war zuvor schon da;
Denn Gottes Nein begleitet Gottes Ja.
Ihr fragt: war Gott zuerst nicht reine Milde?
Des Zornes Möglichkeit war auch im Bilde.

And God's anger – it was already there;
For God's No accompanies God's Yes.
You ask: is God not first and foremost Mercy?
The possibility of anger is also in the picture.

(*Songs without Names II*-LXXII)

Das Gottgedenken muss den Menschen ändern,
Denn zum Beleuchten gibt die Lampe Licht;
Wenn unsre Seele nicht verbessert wird,
Dann zählt das Sprechen frommer Formeln nicht.

Lass ab von falscher Größe — werde klein
Und selbstlos, und du wirst im Himmel sein.

God-remembrance must change man,
For the purpose of a lamp is to give light;
If our soul is not improved,
Then reciting pious formulas is of no avail.

Renounce false greatness – become small
And selfless, and thou wilt be in Heaven.

(*Songs without Names IV*-II)

Our human smallness is exposed without pity:

Lärmendes Nichts ist manche Menschenseel —
Was bläht sie sich, als wär sie gottgeboren?
Ein kurzer Erdentraum voll Eitelkeit,
Ruhloses Tun — und alles ist verloren.

Besinnet euch: seid klein, denn Gott ist groß.
Er hat euch eine Heimat zubereitet
Im Himmelreich: ein goldner Zufluchtsort —
Wohl dem, der gegen seine Seele streitet!

Many a human soul is a noisy void —
Why is she inflated as if born of God?
A brief earthly dream, full of vanity,
Restless activity — and all is lost.

Remember: be small, for God is great.
He has prepared for you a homeland
In the Kingdom of Heaven, a golden shelter —
Blessèd is he who fights against his soul!

(*Adastra*, "Smallness")

Again and again, the poems return to the perplexing and agonizing problem of evil:

Da wo das Lichte erscheinet,
Da muss auch das Finstere drohen;
Wundre und gräme dich nicht;
So will es das wirkende Sein.
Siehe, die niederen Mächte
Bekämpfen heimtückisch die hohen;
Da wo ein Abel erstrahlet,
Da ist auch ein finsterer Kain.

Denn die Allmöglichkeit Gottes
Erfordert ja auch die Verneinung:
Wahrheit und Friede sind himmlisch,
Irdisch sind Falschheit und Krieg.
Ohne das Übel der Trennung,
Wo wäre das Gut der Verneinung?

Ohne der Finsternis Treiben,
Wo wäre der Trost und der Sieg?

Wherever light appears
Darkness must also threaten;
Do not wonder and grieve,
Existence will have it thus.
See how the lower powers
Maliciously battle the higher;
Wherever Abel shines,
There also is dark Cain.

For God's All-Possibility
Also demands negation:
Truth and Peace are of Heaven,
Earthly are falsehood and war.
Without the evil of separation,
Where would be the good of reunion?
Without the work of darkness,
Where would be solace and victory?

(*Adastra*, "Cosmos")

No translation can possibly do full justice to the "poetry"—the meter, rhyme, verbal appositeness, allusions, music, inspiration—of the original German. Each German poem is a diamond—sparkling and clear, an architectural masterpiece full of light.

In his rich profusion of references to the many and varied cultural forms of Europe and beyond—the streets of the Latin Quarter, Andalusian nights, the Virgen del Pilar, the Macarena, sages such as Dante, Shankara, Pythagoras and Plato, the Psalms of David, Arab wisdom, the graces of the Bodhisattvas, Tibetan prayer-wheels, Samurai and Shinto, the songs of love and longing of many peoples—in all of these diverse cultures, Schuon captures the timeless message of truth and beauty which each contains, and renders it present in a most joyful way. When these cultural forms happen to be ones that the reader himself has known and loved, the joy that emanates from the poems is great indeed.

Schuon's long cycle of poems has already been compared to Rumi's *Mathnāwī*. I think that many of his poems can also be compared to the Psalms of David: they are an expression of nostalgia, of mankind's longing for, and ultimate satisfaction in, the Lord. Their main theme is trustful prayer to an ever-merciful God, and benevolence towards men of goodwill. First and foremost, the poems are instruments of instruction. As such, they are a powerful propulsion towards the inward.

A blessing lies not only in the quality of the poems, but also in the quantity—they constitute an all-inclusive totality. On the one hand, Schuon's German poems recapitulate the teachings contained in his philosophical works in French; on the other, they are an inexhaustible, and ever new, purifying fountain—a crystalline and living expression of the *Religio perennis*. They epitomize truth, beauty, and salvation.

—William Stoddart

Translator's Note

Schuon considered his poems didactic in nature and termed them "Sinngedichte," or teaching poems. With this in mind, the aim of the present English edition is to provide a literal rendering of the German text that remains as true as possible to the author's meaning. These translations are the work of William Stoddart, in collaboration with Catherine Schuon and Tamara Pollack. The translations draw extensively on Schuon's own informal, dictated translations. For a full appreciation of the lyrical resonance and musicality of the original, the reader is referred to the several German editions of these poems currently available.[1]

The last nineteen of these twenty-three collections are grouped under two primary headings, *Songs without Names I-XII* and *World Wheel I-VII.* The chronological order in which these collections were written, spanning three years from 1995-1998, is as follows: *Adastra, Stella Maris, Autumn Leaves, The Ring, Songs without Names I-V, World Wheel I, Songs without Names VI-XII,* and *World Wheel II-VII.*

[1] The complete German text of these poems is available in ten volumes from Editions Les Sept Flèches, 1062 Sottens, Suisse, www.sept-fleches.com, as a bilingual German/French edition. A complete bilingual German/Spanish edition is in preparation for 2007 from José J. de Olañeta, Editor, Palma de Mallorca, Spain. Selections can also be found in: *Liebe, Leben, Glück,* and *Sinn* (Freiburg im Breisgau: Verlag Herder, 1997); *Songs for a Spiritual Traveler* (Bloomington: World Wisdom, 2002); and *Adastra & Stella Maris: Poems by Frithjof Schuon* (Bloomington: World Wisdom, 2003).

Songs without Names

Seventh Collection

Certitude, Serenity.
With Certainty comes
Trust in God; Serenity
Brings patience, resignation.

Songs without Names

Seventh Collection

I

Heaven and earth shall pass away,
But my words shall not pass away,
Said Jesus. Therefore know: every wise word
Has its eternal place in the Godhead.

II

Whoever, from the starting-point of earthly existence,
Seeks to know the Lord, will see Him
As the quintessence of things which transcends everything
That surrounds us in the outer world,
And which, at the same time, reveals itself in the Intellect.

God knows Himself in His Being —
But how does He manifest Himself?
In Revelation, in the Pure Intellect,
And in the outward beauty and inward harmony of creatures.
In every noble thing, thou wilt find the trace of God.

III

There are points of view — thou see'st a tree
From where thou standest, and canst not do otherwise;
And there are aspects — form is not color;
The existential dream of things is multiform.

Likewise in the spiritual realm:
There is the nature of Being, and the gaze of the Intellect.
Blessèd the man who sees not merely the play of diversity,
But sees the One with his Heart.

IV

Sometimes one would like to re-live something
That one previously did, and improve one's deed;
It is not worth the trouble; one should not
Dilute the soul's burden with wishful thinking.

As Eckhart said: If thy state before God is good,
Then let past things rest.
As sins, thou may'st regret them –
But not as destiny, for they had to be.

V

For the sage, this earthly life is both
Harder and easier than it is for others:
Harder, because he has a celestial nature;
Easier, precisely because of the consolation this affords –
And because he sees that all things praise the Creator.
Blessèd be he who honors God in the sage.

VI

The Ten Commandments and the Psalms of David –
Therein lies the Old Testament.
And then Jesus' Sermon on the Mount –
One of the most beautiful things known to mankind.
And then the Purification Sura
In the Koran, and the attestation of faith –
Thus the One God, ever anew, has brought
For each branch of humanity, salvation for all souls.

VII

Certitude, Serenity.
With Certitude comes
Trust in God; Serenity
Brings patience, resignation —
This is thy presence before God.

I must also mention fervor and devotion;
Two candles burning before the altar —
Two flames, but before God one single light.

VIII

The tree beside my house was fiery-red
Last autumn; now it is bright gold.
This is the play of nature's angels;
Be ye all welcome — play as ye will.

Red is love, gold is joy —
In each of its garments, the forest gladdens the soul.
So also in winter: its garment is snow —
A white paradise as far as I can see.

In Heaven there are hardly seasons
In our sense, but possibilities of beauty
United in light, in the Majesty of the All-One.

IX

The meeting with God is certitude and peace;
The themes of meditation are the keys.
If thou hast the right key, thou art happy —
The Most High will manifest His goodness to thee.

X

Only God is good, said Jesus. This means
That the worth of the saint and the sage belongs to the Lord.
"Guru is Brahma" does not mean that the man is God —
It means that, from afar, God gives Himself to man.

Only God is good — this is true and also not true;
But the emphasis is on the Divinity.

XI

The Scripture has but little praise for Mary —
For her, whom God placed on the throne of Heaven.
Certainly, if one links Mary with *Māyā*,
It is obvious that she does not reach *Ātmā* .
Nevertheless: if one looks at *Ātmā* in *Māyā*,
Then she is the shining bride of the Sovereign Good.

The ray that refracts on the water's surface
Creates an image, but it is the same light.

XII

Space is infinite insofar as it has
No known limits; but it is round,
Insofar as it is not within God's Being;
Roundness manifests the highest origin.

If space is an image of the Godhead,
Then the sphere is like existence,
Which is perfect, but must have limits;
Roundness is the divine measure of the universe.

So it is with the messenger of God;
He is like the wheel of the sun.
Infinite is
He who created the sun — infinite is the Lord.

XIII

A word from Black Elk, the Red sage:
The Great Spirit always works in circles.
Look around thee – see how the horizon is round;
Thou canst never reach to its end.

XIV

In life one must make many experiences –
Experience is the best medicine.
If one only wants to live and not to learn anything,
Then the dignity of existence is lost.
I say this because learning may be difficult –
Compared to wisdom, the price to pay is small.

XV

Point, straight line, curved line, circle, spiral –
These are symbols of our world
And its becoming; then of the whole work,
Which contains the possibility of all existing things.

The circle: its whole image, the world in itself;
Then the spiral: the world proceeding forward –
Its movement towards its principle within time,
Or else: the world that flees from its own illusion

In its dream of infinity.

XVI

The triangle is an image of the ability
To return to a point of departure:
The direction changes, as if it would
Respect only that which it was at the beginning.

So too may be the life of a man:
Truth, error; then the desire to be liberated.

But the triangle also has a totally different meaning –
Every ternary lies within it:
The triangle is one that wishes to repeat itself in two;
And it is duality, striving towards the One.

XVII

The silent dreaming of our earthly soul
Is like a lyre that sings of longing –
Who knows why, by night and day,
This longing sings in our breast.

It is not because of the perfidy of evil powers,
But because even the wise man has a burden to bear
And, in this world, longs for the Kingdom of God –

Which nevertheless enters deeply into his soul.

XVIII

Fray Gerónimo de la Madre de Dios understood
That the Name of the Lord is the garment of His nearness.
So he called on the Most High with a thirsty soul –
The presence of God lies within our reach,

Because He wills it thus. He looks towards us,
And in our prayer is His Kingdom.

XIX

San Bernardino of Siena taught the people
What the Name of the Lord should mean for them:
It is what ye can read in Holy Scripture –
So gaze on its sign, for it can save you.

Life rushes past, one image after another –
Let the Sign of the Lord be your sword and your shield.

XX

Life – a path, not a standing still:
Life means always to write something new and better.
Take care that thy soul lose nothing –
And that the Most High guide thy pen.

XXI

In principle, God's door is open;
It can be closed, when we are closed
To His will and do not know ourselves –
When we separate ourselves from the Sovereign Good.

Blessèd the man who knows his own weakness,
And with complete trust flees to the All-Merciful.

XXII

Only one human being stands before God and invokes Him,
And all humanity is contained within this one;
Thou canst unite all the prayers of this world
In the invocation of thy heart.

All in one — time is like this too;
What is a day, what is one's whole life?
Stand before God with all thy striving,
Then thy poor now becomes eternity.

XXIII

Outside by the forest
A waterfall rushes;
The birds in the sky are singing,
Lark and nightingale.

The cascading water tells us:
Thus it is with God's power;
The Lord always remains the same,
Yet He ever creates anew.

The birds in the sky sing —
For where the circle
Of God's miracle closes,
Thou hearest praise of God.

The water always renews itself,
While remaining the same element —
This is what a sage
Would call a miracle of God.

What is the enigma of becoming?
It is that a thing in its suchness
Can nonetheless, without changing,
Escape from its own Being.

XXIV

When the Lord God shines into the naught,
Then there must also be broken things;
God gives the naught an existence, and this means:
Existing things must live deep in darkness

For a brief moment of time — like empty foam
In the limitless space of blissful Light.

XXV

"Verily, My mercy precedeth
My wrath." It cannot be otherwise:
Without the world, Allah's wrath would not be;
Without the wrath, what would there be to pardon?

XXVI

What is the naught? It has reality only
As a tendency to corrupt the Good;
There is no naught in itself; what does not exist
Cannot have a consequence, and cannot inherit anything.

The tendency to corrupt can be defined:
You can see inward nothingness in the form of pride.
Where there are good qualities, there is Being —
On a shining ray from Being, the soul can be happy.

XXVII

The Absolute — what a magical word:
A word that could kill a soul
And resurrect it. It is God's nearness and power —
Within thy depths and in all thy needs.

XXVIII

The most beautiful things that the Most High created
Are nature, poetry, music, and woman;
Then also the sanctuary — made by human hands —
Where the happiness of the Spirit blossoms.

Music, poetry and woman; according to Plato,
They are the most noble things that thou canst see or hear;
Half earth, half heaven.
Woman is the God-created body of beatitude.

XXIX

Reality, Truth; Beauty and Love:
If nothing else remained to me,
I would still be happy, great or small,
To be safe in God's Hands.

XXX

Just as a mill wheel turns by day,
And after work is done keeps still,
So it is with the play of thoughts —
Be silent at the right moment in order to thank God.

XXXI

It may happen that thou art tired,
Because the world has stolen thy whole day.
Strive not to understand the absurd —
God knows best what has made thee tired.

XXXII

Every kind of consolation is unworthy weakness,
A philosopher told me, who was angry about the psyche.
The fool, who places himself above everything, does not know
That consciousness of God contains every consolation.

XXXIII

In Vrindāvan — Krishna and Rādhā's swing,
Adorned with flowers, dances up and down —
Half earthly and half heavenly movement
Which gave Krishna's *gopis* a sweet blessing.

What can be the meaning of this play?
That the wondrous nearness of God
Is linked with childlikeness of soul —
And with God's smile of grace, eternally.

Ātmā and *Māyā* — *Ātmā* is *Māyā*'s goal;
Truth lives in love's eternal play.

XXXIV

There is a naught that is all — I mean
The death of the soul in the Lord.
And an all that is a naught — such I would like to call
The universe woven of dreams.

An old wise saying tells us:
"Blessèd the man who dies before he dies,
For he dies not when he dies";
He receives his true self
From the fountain of immortality.

XXXV

"A mighty fortress is our God" –
So be strong in the power of faith.
Faith is knocking on God's door –
And faith has opened it.

For if there were no longing,
There could be no "yes" from God.
"Man lives not by bread alone,"
But by each Word from out God's Being.

XXXVI

Vacare Deo – austerity or sweetness
Can be the soul's attitude before the Lord.
It is *vairāgya* when it is austere;
But if it is sweet, it is a blessèd wine.

Vairāgya – holy impassibility, motionless –
And beatitude, nurtured by love.

XXXVII

I take refuge in God
From the world and from the soul;
For what I should, I cannot be –
Only the Self is without flaw.

When God created us human beings,
It was as if He said:
Be what ye are; for what I want
Is to hear your call.

Two things man must be at once:
Great in spirit and small in earthly play.

XXXVIII

God's Truth and God's Presence.
To these man's answer is certitude
And peace of soul; then resignation
Combined with trust in God's Goodness.

Thou knowest that the door is open to thee,
Though the whole world were to collapse –
Do not say that life's duties are too hard.
Thou knowest the way to the Lord; what more dost thou want?

XXXIX

"*Pues tanto a mi Amado quiero,*
que muero porque no muero."
Thus spoke Teresa: I die because
I cannot die for my beloved.

And so the Madre loved death,
Which gives us eternity and life.

XL

In the early morning, in the clear sky,
Shines the *Stella Matutina* which reminds me
Of the encounter that my heart experienced;
I had never dreamt of such a miracle –

Heaven's Goodness brought me, on the sea,
A draught that opened up a world.

XLI

The pious man, it is said, is always in a good state —
There is the Truth, which shines from above;
Also, he knows himself to be under God's protection,
In this world woven of pleasure and pain.

Twofold is the consolation given by God:
In time, and also for eternal life.

XLII

The point of departure is pure metaphysics,
As it is understood by Shankara's Vedantic doctrine;
But do not think that every other school
That teaches something similar is on the same level.

Thou canst read the Truth in several Scriptures,
But thy heart also contains Its deepest essence.

XLIV

Unity has two sides: one-and-onliness
In the unlimited space of possibility;
And union, identity — the most profoundly inward,
Where possibilities merge into the One.

XLV

When a messiah comes, one needs the theory
That the human world is hopelessly corrupted.

But where pure Truth shines, it is clear
The heart has reached what dwells within it.

XLVI

If people say false and bad things about thee,
And underestimate thee, be not concerned —
Let them be what they are — if they hurt thee,
They cannot bring it with them into God's House.

When people say true and good things about thee,
Then it is true, despite thy humility.
God will reward them for their action;
Thy heart should be what it was before their praise.

For God's approbation thou shouldst strive —
Without scorning the judgement of good people.

XLVII

Even if the Master commits a sin,
The disciple does not have the right to criticize him.
The disciple must be in submission as before —
The magical power of faith must suffice him.
It may be that the act done by the Master
Has nothing to do with the sin of the ignorant.

This a great Sufi Shaikh has written —
One should love the divine within the sage.

XLVIII

Let us be on Jacob's shining ladder,
That leads from earthly night to Paradise;
High in the sunshine of God's Truth,
Far from the folly that freezes the heart.

XLIX

Passion that glows like a fire
Is often accompanied by the frost of selfishness;
The soul needs self-domination,
And the noble fare of magnanimity.

Hell burns, but its deepest circle —
Dante said — is solid ice.

Where there is love, there must also be wisdom;
Where there is strength, the victor must often forgive.

L

Peasants write above their door:
"Everything is dependent on God's blessing."
And: "Blessèd be those
Who come in and out of this house."

The blessing is the sacred air
That brings to life the fragrance of Heaven.
God has painted us an image of this
In the rainbow that shines in the sky.

LI

"Great God, we praise Thee" —
What does it mean to praise God?
That everything good that thou knowest
In existence, comes from above.

The Lord, in whose Goodness thou trustest,
Will prepare for thee a bed of grace;
And when thou devoutly lookest toward Him,
Thy faith will save thee.

LII

The prohibition of images by Jews and Moslems means:
The Lord alone is Creator.
But others think: man is made in the image of God,
So man too must be a creator of images.

Man's art is either a symbol
That brings us something of the heavenly worlds;
Or a consolation, which, in the earthly world,
Sings a song of Truth and Beauty.

LIII

With the Most High I wish to be; in my soul
It is almost dark; I have a longing
Like the thirsting hart in David's psalm.
Be still, my heart: God also wants to be with me.

Man and God: the reciprocity
Between the wheel of time and Eternity.

LIV

Thou art born from the breath of the Lord;
This is man's meaning and essential destiny.
The star of the Spirit leads thee towards the Most High —
Go thy way, O heart, do not look back.

Thou art indeed conscious of the past —
But thy breast shows thee the path to God.
In knowledge the circle closes —
Blessèd is he who knows this in his heart.

That thou art born from the breath of the Most High
Means that thou art free, and of the chosen.

LV

What is man? Firstly, he is knowledge:
The light of the Spirit rends *Māyā*'s illusion.

Then the nature of man is action —
Blessèd the man who has found God's Word.

And then man's nature is faith —
The soul presses the grapes of salvation.

Finally I would mention Identity:
Man must recognize Divine Being in his heart.

LVI

There are two possibilities when a man experiences
Within himself something of creative value:
Either he is inflated with a vain self-satisfaction,
Or his heart is turned towards God.

Man must flee from the euphoria of the ego:
Either outward, or deep within himself.

LVII

Be very careful, when thou complainest —
For, in God's eyes, it could be a lack of gratitude.
He hears thee, so ponder what thou sayest —
The soul should be free from bitterness.

If injustice or foolishness wounds thee —
Do not forget all that God has given thee.

LVIII

When the Indian speaks of the Great Spirit
In sign-language, his hand describes
A spiral winding upward –
The image replaces discursive reason.

The relationship between God and the world
Is not a straight line, it is a play –
Rising from the to-and-fro of things
To the Absolute, the goal of all existence.

LIX

With Christians, sentiment is ascetic,
With Hindus, it is esthetic, and even erotic.
Yin-Yang: there are also possibilities in between,
But they do not lessen the oppositions.

Christian sentiment readily sees sin
Where beauty and love are blossoming.
The Hindu feels that, where the symbol speaks,
The world will be forgiven to the one who understands it.

LX

Truth and beauty go together:
What is divinely true, radiates beauty;
The beautiful and the noble bear witness to the truth;
The sacred is God's bouquet of flowers.

Only the fool sees nothing beautiful in the doctrine
And gives not to beauty the honor of wisdom.
One could exaggerate the rights of beauty –
But one should not call it an empty illusion.

LXI

How canst thou avoid pettiness entirely
In a world that forces thee towards small things?
Take care that when faced by trivialities, thou remainest strong,
Until the Most High grants thee something better –

Until He reminds thee of the greatness
Of the God-consciousness that resounds in thy heart,
And releases thee from the emptiness of everyday turmoil.

LXII

Smallness in greatness means: when a great man
Shows himself petty in a certain action;
Greatness in smallness means: when an average man,
In a fate that is his, inclines toward greatness.

Caesar was great, yet he was small in his behavior
When Vercingetorix surrendered;
A nameless nobody is small and gray,
But in battle, he can attain the heroic.

LXIII

Tantric dance – you think it is merely sensuous and earthly,
Not spiritual and heavenly; but the two are woven together.
The naked dancers express thanks to their God –
And likewise the witnesses, who praise the Creator of beauty
As they contemplate this splendor made by God.

The power of beauty is interiorizing.

LXIV

I am the great peace after the storm,
After the wild melody of the world-sea —
Say: peace, peace; O heart, thou art the Self —

Om, shanti, shanti; aham Brahmāsmi.

LXV

Differences of opinion among the doctors of the law,
Are a blessing from God, it is said in Islam.
Why? Because the light of the spiritual miracles
That move the heart is inexhaustible.

Our soul too is multiform
In its simplicity. God is One;
And every truth that comes from above,
Whatever be its form, belongs to God.

If God did not wish to dwell in a variety of hearts
Here below, there would be no religions.

LXVI

For Hindus, he is the Jagadguru;
For Moslems, he is the *Qutb*, the Pole.
Many a seeker would like to find his way
To this Master of Masters.
His lofty words are heavenly in nature;
His trace shines forth in many teachings.

Where does he live, this sage of all the world?
He lives in the Spirit that the Lord hath chosen.

LXVII

God is the Outward and the Inward –
Thus teaches the Koran. So must the soul
Combine within itself a mountain top
And its deep, invisible cavern.

In the Outward, where beauty unfolds,
Thou must devoutly behold thy Creator;
In the deep Inward, where the Divine Spirit reigns,
Thine illumined heart must understand the Self.

In Heaven too, where dwell the blessèd,
There must be an Outward and an Inward.
But finally duality will be unity,
Without any loss – how is known by God alone.

The thousand Names that are the Lord's –
Remain as Being, within the silence of His Beyond-Being.

LXVIII

God is the First and the Last,
Teaches the Koran: for God, the Creator,
Was there before the world was. He is the Lord,
When the whole world falls into nothingness.

A yet deeper truth: the ground of Beyond-Being exists
Before Being, the Creator God,
With Whom we men can speak.
For *Ātmā* is Reality, and *Māyā* but appearance.

LXIX

Why art thou the happiest of men?
Forget not to think of this:
Thou hast the Truth, and the Way of Truth –
Be grateful; thou canst have nothing better.

LXX

The bliss of trust: *a priori*, mistrust is
Foreign to the good man —
And to the childlike soul that is readily ashamed
Of every temptation to bad will,

Experience helps, but so does sharp discrimination;
May the Most High grant us His support.

LXXI

Calumny by definition always goes too far;
Too far? It can, it seems to me, go much further
Than merely too far. What can the will of Heaven be?
One would like to know the profound reason.
Patience, O my heart, and gratitude; be at peace.

Let the universe have its possibilities —
And may God direct the poor soul.

LXXII

Many of the charms of the bodies of beautiful women —
Given life by nobility of soul —
Are like consolations from Heaven;
Beauty can build for us a bridge to the Most High.

Thus can our soul look inward,
And free itself from the spell of desire.

LXXIII

It is so hard that thou must be a rock
For all others,
And that nonetheless thou must sometimes suffer
In thy life's journey —

Like all men, yet without being
Like all the weak ones.
Be thou then a rock, for thou art not alone —
The Lord will watch over thee.

LXXIV

The Name Allah is sometimes prolonged
In *Allāhumma* — as if one wanted to combine
The Name Allah with *Om;*
Two spiritual worlds on the same track.

Om is like *Shūnyamūrti,* it is the form
Of the Formless — the norm of all Divine Names;
Beyond-Being has put itself into the Word.

LXXV

Priest, warrior, merchant, servant —
Far below these four comes the one without caste;
Everyone is confined within his station —
Thus does the goddess of destiny cast her lots.

Over them all is the man who is above caste,
Paramahamsa, who is bound by no duty of station —
And who, from his God-willed height,
Proclaims the limitless ray of Truth.

LXXVI

In a world where everything is ugly
For the first time in history,
One cannot ask a wise man
To renounce the solace of recreation.

All the sages of the past
Lived in beauty; for there was nothing else
In lands where Revelation dominated –
And with this, the sense of God and bliss.

LXXVII

Truth and patience; the Koran links
These two treasures, when it says:
Lost is he who does not possess them in his heart;
For only through them are souls reborn.

With patience hold fast to the truth –
This is the way that cancels the debt of existence.

LXXVIII

What separates us from the Most High is like a mountain
That we must overcome with our own hands.
So we start digging, but there is too much earth;
We stand before heavy and gigantic walls

And we continue digging, for we must
In order to be free. Until we see:
The mountain was but a dream. The truth is
That illusion alone can separate us from the Sovereign Good.

LXXIX

Moses crossed the Red Sea
With his children of Israel. In like manner
The souls of the pious cross the flood of existence,
From the one shore to the blissful other.

Pharaoh, who drowned in the flood,
Is he who is sunk in earthly illusion;
Blessèd is he who escapes this baleful illusion.

Mount Sinaï: the gratitude of the free heart
Which, after trials, attains to God's Word.

LXXX

Daily meditation is a must,
Otherwise we will end up knowing nothing.
Whoever gains not, loses; whoever has seed,
Must sow it — the seed will be grateful.

LXXXI

According to some theologians,
A conversion resulting from the threat of hell is worthless;
But others say that conversion is conversion —
Heaven never betrays hope.

This has been applied to the case of Pharoah,
Who, on Moses' trail, converted at the last moment;
There was no stubborn theologian there
To refuse the poor sinner this final consolation.

LXXXII

A sin against the Holy Spirit, said Jesus,
Will never be forgiven. This is the sin
That knows no conversion, for it surrounds
The heart with a layer of ice.

In this state, one wishes to know nothing of the naked Truth,
And one tramples under foot whatever Truth may say.
Compassion awaits behind closed doors –
God does not save those who wish to lose themselves.

Blessèd the man who understands the nature of the Holy Spirit –
Who separates the core of his soul from pride.

LXXXIII

What Paul taught in his epistle to the Corinthians
About love, is the Holy Spirit –
God's nature, which shows mankind,
With shining hand, the way to Heaven.

LXXXIV

The soul's peace in God is unconditional –
It does not depend on life's moods.
When Primal Truth resounds in our consciousness,
God's blessing descends into the heart.

The guests of Existence come in and out,
Pure Being remains faithful to Itself –

The nature of God, that sings of Peace.

LXXXV

How can human beings live together for so long
Without noticing what it is to be a human being:
There is an I, a thou; surroundings: space and time —
The I cannot rise above itself,

Above the illusion of its uniqueness.
Most people — blinded by everyday life — do not see
That we are mirrors of the All-One.

LXXXVI

The greatest vice that corrupts the soul
Is pride, as every religion teaches.

Deadly deceit in the human mind
Is to despair of the Most High's Mercy.

LXXXVII

When my late father lay dying,
He looked unwaveringly
At a passage from holy Scripture
On the wall facing him;
"The Lord is my shepherd" — David's psalm.
Painful is earthly death;
But celestial was my father's end —
He met his God.

LXXXVIII

In my youth, I wandered over fields,
And liked to withdraw into silent forests –
I knew nothing of my future,
But I felt that something had to come.

In the wheel of time, there was no profit –
In my heart, I sought the meaning of my human state.

LXXXIX

The *Avatāra*, the prophet, the master –
God has given a Word to different human manifestations
To distribute according to people's needs;
Without the bread of God, no humanity can live.

It is distributed according to earthly need –
The bread of Heaven ripens in the one who spreads the Word.

XC

The pilgrim journeys faithfully towards his goal –
He takes joy already in the distant sanctuary.
He is not daunted by the hardships of the way –
He travels on and he does not look back;
He climbs patiently over many hills –
His joy in the sacred lends him wings.

Be thou the pilgrim, who makes his way through life
And yet stands motionless before the Highest.
Movement is the way of earthly life;
But God with His Grace is immutable.

XCI

The consolation that makes life easier
Is that we walk in God, and are able to do so;
The goal is already present in the "now" — illusion vanishes.

Faith is: to recognize that the light that may escape us
Is nevertheless the radiation of God —
When our earthly soul cannot see,
Nonetheless to have faith in the Holy Spirit within us.

XCII

Life is a garment, and every man
Has only his own. But his deep being
Stands naked before God, ready for eternity —
God says to this inner being: thou art mine.

Life is man's free will;
But what the Creator's profound intention made
Is man's eternal vocation —
Whatever be the meaning of his earthly husk.

XCIII

The mystery of disappointment. Dost thou not feel
That thy soul lacks insight?
Many things may be worse than thou didst expect —
Think not of this; let thy heart be pure.

The world must be — earth is earth;
So dream not that it should be otherwise.

XCIV

If God is purity, I am sobriety;
If God is power, I will cultivate the best of acts;
If God is the treasure, I am contentment;
If God is salvation, I will trust in Him.

If God alone is real, the world cannot be;
If God is Identity, then He is mine.

XCV

Stern man is strength and knowledge;
Sweet woman is beauty and love.
The radiance of man is in his intellect;
The primordial image of femininity is a beautiful body —
To which noble sentiment shows the highest respect.

Masculine and feminine: each is One human being.
As friends, they are equals; as sexes, they are
Lord and helper, two modes of duty.
Then again, adoration from pole to pole —
God and goddess; each reigns in his own way.

XCVI

He brought light from Heaven, but faced difficulties
In the realm of everyday life. Light, because
The Word of the Most High filled his heart, but in this world.
He was indeed radiation, but he was also earth.

XCVII

There is perfection in this world;
But remember: this perfection is not the same
As that of the Most High, for: "Only God is good."
An earthly value does not belong to Heaven's realm.

In this world, one can say many things,
But often wonders if one should dare to speak.

XCVIII

"Blessings and peace": the Moslem salutation.
I think of the Tree of Paradise:
Certitude in the depths of the heart,
And serenity in the realm of thought.

The root and the crown of the Tree of the Spirit;
That the soul may dwell in the inmost Self, near the Most High.

XCIX

Ingratitude: the world's reward, according to proverb.
One gives the best, and gives it willingly.
Who would not like to receive a good answer?

The best answer is thanks from the Lord.

C

The core of primordial prayer: God's Name
Is the guarantee of certain salvation,
If thou art patient in faith. As seen by God,
The way is easy, but human effort is steep.

CI

Wisdom regarding phenomena
Is the perception — by the Intellect — of the essences
Or archetypes. Only what is good allows us
To break through the walls of appearance.

In the case of the bad, there is no archetype;
Bad is merely privation, not manifestation of Being —
It shows the traces of nothingness in the realm of existence.

So maintain thy connection with the radiation of Being:
Be thou the archetype of thine own existence;
Before God thy husk is of no importance.

CII

Why is there existence? — that is the question.
Why is there not just nothing? Because Being
It is the necessity to be: because one thing was created,
Then two things, yea, the whole expanse of the universe.

Possibility burst into nothingness:
This is the cause that we call Creator —
And someone had to be there, in order to know it.

CIII

In a world where there is beauty, there must
Also be ugliness; but with God
It is not so — there are no contradictions
In Heaven's realm, in the Divine Ipseity.

When God's radiation fills man's soul,
There is beauty therein without any opposite —
The Good in itself shines eternally.

CIV

It is said that God's Spirit is beyond good and evil –
That in It there is neither good nor bad.
This is not so. God is indeed without contradiction;
But this means: He is all that is positive.

"Yes" is not simply the opposite of "no" –
"Yes" is in itself, it is Pure Being.

CV

A man loves this, but should love that;
He looks longingly on values that are doubtful.
He should, before God, banish his dreaming ego;
God knows what everyone, who knows himself, should love.

CVI

He who has important duties, also has the rights
That correspond to his responsibility;
Likewise, there are no rights without duties –
The nature of things proclaims this relationship.
Dreaming is of no use here, because the Lord will judge.

CVII

Artistic beauty is a cosmic power
That has often brought heaven to earth.
The man who serves it may not be spiritual –
The interiorizing wine flows for others.
Here I think especially of music –
It brings the wise back to their own hearts.

CVIII

The artist, it has been said, is like a spring
That gushes forth untroubled by reflection;
This is not so. For true art demands
Everything that pertains to man.

Ars sine scientia nihil. Human art
Does not simply burst out like the instinct of animals;
If thou wishest only to create joyously and without thinking,
Thou hast nothing to give to others.

CIX

Old age is the winter of life;
It likes to re-awaken what once was,
Yet on the other hand, all the past
Is covered with the serenity of snow.
An image of Pure Being, as far as I can see —
Flowers are dreaming underneath deep snow.

CX

There is no time in the nature of God,
Nor in the encounter with the Lord.
The moment of prayer is eternity —
It stands in the sky like the morning star;
In the now of the heart lies thy whole life.

CXI

The sage is more naïve than fools
Within the space of life, where everything is changing —
Because he sees the things around him
As archetypes, and treats them as such.
That he is at the same time more intelligent —
The foolish world cannot easily understand.

CXII

The conqueror, proud with his courageous legions,
Comes home to Rome – center of the world –
On a chariot decorated for triumph;
Near him stands one, who bows to him and says:
"Forget not, O hero, that thou too art mortal."

CXIII

When Alexander, master of the entire Greek world,
Asked Diogenes what his wishes were,
Diogenes said: "Move out of my sunlight" –
He was not one who easily complained.

Selfhood in the Godhead is the wise man's bliss.

CXIV

Hindus like to have in their names
The word *ānanda* – "highest bliss."
Ānanda is the quintessence of the soul
Which, through truth, has freed itself from illusion;
Through truth: for the deepest nature of happiness
Is *Brahma satyam.*
Many things may make us happy –
And give us joy – but only one thing can deliver us.

CXV

If thou sayest certitude, thou thinkest of the depth
Within thy breast; if thou sayest serenity,
Thou thinkest of the heavenly space within thy forehead –
Of silence, of floating in the realm of eternal snow.

The Absolute; the Infinite.

CXVI

Motion, motionlessness; and the passage from one to the other –
Something absolute, neither one nor the other;
So it is also with that which lies between mere earthly thought
And the remembrance of God, wherein is a discerning of spirits:
An entrance of God into the flux of the world –
An instant that contains eternity.

CXVII

With each of the poems, I think:
This one may be the last. Not because I will it,
But because God could will it. Mine is what comes to me;
And one day, my pen will be still.

It is strange that I should think of saying this;
On the one hand, it is evident;
On the other hand, destiny brews what it can –
What my wishes are, you should not ask.

CXVIII

It is said that God created the vast world
Out of nothing; that it is His shadow –
Neither reality nor its opposite;
Other than God – yet faithful to His nature.

The universe had to be, because the Good
Rested still unknown in God's silence –
And so creation's melody rang out.

CXIX

Worldly creativity — because people flee
From God and from themselves. Give heed,
Stand still! And pay your debt to the Most High —
Then He will watch over everything else.

CXX

For Jesus, the Divine Creator was the Father;
He himself, the *Avatāra*, was the Son —
And God within man was the Holy Ghost;
Salvation, Heaven, was the reward of faith.
What Jesus said was for him experience:
He himself was the Word, the Book, the Revelation.

What came after him, was not the "I" of a messiah;
Islam came as religion as such
And was the final form of the first *Dharma*.
Every Word of God is a norm of life.

CXXI

Bhakti and *jñāna*: mystical experience
Is like an image that enraptures our soul;
On the contrary, the idea of the gnostic
Is a consciousness that hearkens to the truth.
Ecstasy, which is overwhelming like wine,
Can, in the realm of gnosis, be sober.

CXXII

The angel called her "full of grace";
"What manner of greeting" — asked Mary — "is this?"
Then she felt: "Be it done unto me according to thy word" —
And was filled with the Spirit, with the Kingdom of Heaven.
Humble she was, and did not believe easily —
And she was chosen before the Face of God.

CXXIII

Prudence is the mother of all intelligence;
This is often said, but rarely practiced.
So let prudence make our faith more wise —
Equilibrium is the way of all wisdom.

In every action and experience,
Respice finem — think of the result.

CXXIV

You ask me about space and time,
Infinity and eternity —
Then formal limits and ephemerality;
Form and becoming; number —

The Lord is Beginning, Creator, and End;
You must understand well these categories of existence —
The way from God to God is long.

CXXV

The "now" of the Spirit is: escaping time
For God, through unceasing self-forgetfulness;
The "now" of the fool is: enjoying the world,
At every moment, like an animal.

For every wise support, one can find
Follies that would bind us to nothingness.

It is the same with the "here" in the depth of the heart —
The "here" of the fool is inflaming the ego:
Whatever world and life have to offer belongs to me —
But the end of the story is a different matter.

Truth waits for the scales of the Most High.

CXXVI

With regard to the unknown, the Latin peoples are
More guarded than Germanics;
The Romans remained securely within the Roman domain;
Whereas the Germans readily dreamt of distant shores.

In this is neither blame nor praise;
In every people there are men whom
The intellect raises above sentimental limitations;
There never existed a people without doors.

CXXVII

They think this world is full of sweetness,
While the sage groans in renunciation and darkness,
In this, they say, one will not find
The golden paradise one longs for.
The worldly man does not understand the night of the Spirit –
That Laila dances in a wreath of light.

Thy deepest heart contains the holy shrine,
The naked goddess and the cup of wine.

CXXVIII

She may be dark as is the night,
Yet she is beautiful, as the Lord made her –
Whoso looks on her with the fire of desire
Cannot see her, but her veil alone,
Within whose depths her mystery is waiting.

CXXIX

Thou knowest that thou canst not change the world;
Let things be what they must be.
It is true that there are things we can change,
And others not. Stand thou on both thy feet.

Forget not that the grace of the Highest Good
Can pierce through senseless things;
For God is free, He manifests compassion –
The very essence of Being is Felicity.

CXXX

Audiatur et altera pars —
a saying all too often forgotten.
Even when thou knowest what thou knowest,
thou shouldst hear what the other has to say.
For it may be
that he will tell us something new;
And the peace of justice —
no man of honor will disturb.

CXXXI

When lovers say sweet words to one another —
Think not their speech will entirely pass away.
The words already were, in eternity,
And will remain in the Divine Essence —

Because everything good belongs to God;
If you are good, you will be eternally under His protection.

CXXXII

Logic can be petty — as when it pointlessly
Upholds unimportant things out of a mere sense of duty;
"Let five be even," says the proverb which rightly
Protects the normal man's sense for better and greater things.

On cathedrals there are always small asymmetries;
Eckhart said: in blasphemy there is hidden praise of God —
The imperfect cannot but praise the perfect.

CXXXIII

Poetry can have three origins:
What the poet carries in his soul
Of God-given Knowledge;
Then the spiritual state, placed in his heart
By the Most High.
And finally, some small event,
A nothing. But what counts here
Is whatever helps — grace and the result.

CXXXIV

The outer man is both form and life:
Form is what contains the meaning of things;
Life is the dance of existence, the round of love.
Thus God wished to manifest to men
The wonders of His own Being.

Existence and possibility; figurative art and music.
The truth of the spirit, and the happiness of the soul.

CXXXV

One of the most difficult problems in metaphysics
Is that of possibility; so said
An arch-pedant, who had dissected everything —
And for whom, it seems, there was nothing left to know.

Difficult metaphysical problems do not exist
When thou hast grasped the nature of things;
In pure contemplation there is no conflict.
The question of possibility is easy;
Difficult is only a thinking whose convulsions
Tear everything to pieces and achieve nothing.

CXXXVI

There are truths so precious that
One wants to say them more than once.
Just as, from year to year, the flowers bloom,
So poetry too has a right to repetition.

CXXXVII

There is what we experience in the outward world;
And then what we think within ourselves —
Each is a to-and-fro and an up-and-down;
And may God direct us to the meaning of life.

"Man proposes, God disposes" — man experiences freely,
But on paths that are woven by destiny.

CXXXVIII

Opportet — it is said — *haereses esse;*
And also: *felix culpa.* For evil is quite often
The cause of a good change;
And one who errs without pride becomes better.

It often seems that the world-wheel turns in a bad way.
But essentially its action is right.
The sun gives us the light we need;
Do not complain if it also casts shadows.

CXXXIX

Aglaia, Euphrosyne, and Thalia are
The Graces, that Beatific Being sends to us –
"Splendor," "Happiness," and "Blossoming";
Heaven that turns towards us threefold

As beauty, joy, and love –
So that the evil one darken not our days;
In the Spirit alone is happiness perfected.

CXL

I once met the archbishop of Venice.
I was happy to see the priestly prince
And greeted him. He said: *Benedico te* –
Long did I think of this, as I continued on my way.

CXLI

One would like everything to be in harmony
In our surroundings and in our life.
Too small a desire. There is nothing better
Than to soar spiritually above everything.

CXLII

Sound character and depth of soul,
Honesty, fidelity, and love of wisdom – hence
Also some dreaminess; all in all:
The German is energetic, but also heavy.
The German character contains much that is good;
But one does not wish to praise one's own house.

People are too unforgiving towards the Germans –
One only thinks of what they should have been.

CXLIII

Venice and Florence; then Granada,
Seville and Córdoba; the beauty that dwells
In cities. The melody in stone
Of the Old World. — Not so America,
Where all beauty is blooming in the wilderness,
In forests and prairies, extending to the West —
One senses, in these vast expanses of the Great Spirit,
Processions of Indians riding across the sky,
Which no one will ever see again on earth.

CXLIV

For many, it sounds like a mockery when one says
That the very substance of man is beatitude;
It seems there is all too much suffering in the world —

But all this lies in the dream-world of time.
Beatitude is inward, only the husk
Of man suffers, until illusion is shattered
On the rock of the Highest Power — Eternity.

CXLV

The bright day is greeting us — shining sun,
Wandering clouds, and earthly things
Both still and moving — on the edge
Of possibility.

Then comes the silent night:
Infinity with countless stars
In the blackness of space, in God's deep remoteness.

Holy night, that covers the day like a veil —
Silence of the heart, filled with adoration.

CXLVI

Mā shā'a 'Llāh – "what God has willed" –
Are these words merely the expression of a lazy belief in fate?
Certainly not. They are rigorous, but also mild;
What is, must be; but God is our refuge.

Songs without Names

Eighth Collection

Thou art born from the breath of the Lord;
This is the meaning of man and his destiny.
The star of the Spirit leads thee to the Most High –
Go thy way, O heart, do not look back.

Songs without Names

Eighth Collection

I

The sun, a heavenly image made of gold and light,
A symbol of Being, that rules the world.
And then the silent moon, a silver shield –
Yet it possesses no light of its own.

So the moon is like Existence,
Whose face can only reflect what is unique,
And as the Unique, breaks through the naught.

II

Intellect, and also reason, are like the sun;
The psyche and sentiment are like the moon.
Intellect is day, in it everything is clear;
But the psyche's play lives in the dark.

A symbol is multivalent, and held in honor –
The sacred resounds in all spheres of existence.

III

The Great Absolute – I wish
To say it a thousand times – is more powerful than
All the cares of the soul. In its ray
Illusion disappears, and the heart is safe.

IV

Birth and death: entering the earthly world
Is more painful than leaving the earth.
Understand: birth is also a kind of death;
But death in the Most High shoothes all suffering,

Because Heaven's light receives the soul. God-remembrance
Is also a death — but one in which God will give us His Life:
The Good Shepherd lets us graze in eternity.

V

A kernel of sweetness is to be found in asceticism;
A kernel of rigor, in the noble love
Of earthly beauty. The one who renounces,
Nevertheless lives in beauty; the one who
Loves what earth's nature offers him, must earnestly
Dominate his heart as it strives toward Heaven

VI

There is the difficult question of pleasure and pain —
Earthly man must bear them both:
Pain with patience, and pleasure with dignity;
Pleasure degrades, if it does not comprise renunciation.

Pain imposes, but enjoyment is free;
Commandment: one must be up to its level.

VII

Man is a bundle of experiences which,
Ever growing, flees down the alley of life.
Around him a stream of things, creatures, and dreams,
Without asking, pulls him along
In a direction no one knows —
A path of destiny, at the Most High's behest.

Only one thing is necessary to understand:
That there is a choice: not to love illusion,
But, with God's help, to move towards God —
As the Lord has written it in our heart.

VIII

To give away — to sacrifice something
Belonging to the world of the I;
Instead of hoarding, to make oneself somewhat poorer;
And joyfully to enrich another, unknown soul.

With all peoples and in all times,
There have been celebrations where one gave things away,
And drowned all avarice and egoism
In the noble pleasure of renunciation.

Thou canst not imagine a greater bliss,
Than giving thy whole heart to the Lord.

IX

The ego should know: what I am and what I have
Is not from myself, but is a gift from the Other.
This never occurs to the fool:
If there were no God, there would be no "I am."

X

The symbolism of the tree: it is a protection,
And also, in itself, a joyful sign of life;
An image of the soul, that wishes to grow upwards.

But a tree can reach only the height
Prescribed for it by God; after this it stops.

XI

Hindus, Celts, and Germans honored
The green tree at their great festivals;
They decorated it, and danced around it,
So that the gods would not withhold their favor.
Many phenomena in the world of the Creator
Are for us shrines that contain God's ray.

Then there is also degeneration: idols and golden calves;
Sins against the Most High, and against oneself.

XII

Tagore wanted the soul of India
To awaken to the dignity of free man.
The result was that one considered all that India was,
And ought to be, as a burden.

Man is only man. Only the light of wisdom is wonderful:
Vedanta, and with it Shankara,
Are the adornment of the true India.

XIII

Genius is a problem and not a problem;
For there are highly gifted people without greatness,
And great men without creative gifts.
What is falsely great simply uncovers the shame of littleness.

XIV

For the fool, things are made of stone;
For the spirit of the wise, they are transparent;
The wise spirit sees that everything points towards the One,

From whose Light and from whose Love we are born.

XV

The earth: a sphere without life;
It turns, but its position is tilted;
It revolves round the sun, which also moves
In the miracle of space — the way is without limit.

This may sound like a fairy tale, wonderous;
Do not believe that all this was without forethought.
The world is an incredible poetry of Being —
Is it understandable? Ye do not even understand yourselves.

XVI

At an early age, as life's golden morning dawns,
Knowledge is hammered into children's heads;
The fact is that when children are forced
Into useless knowledge, their souls cannot grow.
I had friends in my early years —
No wonder that because of schoolwork,
They did not grow in spirit; they could still think,
But only with difficulty could they steer the ship of life.

XVII

In compulsory education there is much with which to find fault.
Morocco's beautiful craftsmanship is dying:
The children go to school, and cannot inherit
Their fathers' crafts, so rich in symbolism.
Such is progress — even though the people's heart is breaking.

I do not say that all children are the same;
One of them feels called to what is difficult,
Another does not, but is still of noble spirit.
A people's genius is their kingdom of Heaven —
Remain what ye were a thousand years ago!

XVIII

One of the most difficult things we must learn
Is to accept humiliations with courage:
It may happen that destiny forces us
To be patient and detached;
So let us say yes to the will of God,
And let us accept injustice for love of Him and of ourselves.

XIX

The Name of God; then resignation;
Then trust in God. There is no greater consolation
In earth's misery. And may God
Raise us above the weakness of our human condition.

XX

Be not astonished because of a trial,
For without trials man cannot grow;
Such is human nature, that
God can entirely forgive only the one who has accepted trials.

XXI

Serenitas – soaring above the clouds;
The world is full of hither and thither – and so
Is the human soul. The world and the soul are small
Compared with the sky. If thou wouldst live like an eagle,
Never forget pure and luminous Being.

XXII

The Name is Truth, and Presence of God;
It brings certitude, and trust in God;
Serenity – its echo is resignation;
There is no other way to look on God or the world.

XXIII

What does the doctrine of purgatory tell us?
That heaven does not overlook every imperfection.
Why then does one say that God wishes to forgive us?
This means: if we consecrate ourselves entirely to His path.

The reason why God's doors are open
May seem small – no one can see it.

XXIV

Beethoven's religion was music,
It could be said; but he had faith.
He suffered the heavy soul-anguish of the deaf –
And so his art was his only happiness
Before his God – and no one could take it from him.

The Moonlight Sonata – a melody
That is much more than a mere display of genius.

XXV

Savonarola, preacher and ascetic,
Was right to castigate worldly art,
But not right to oppose good painting;
Art and asceticism are different worlds.
One can criticize many artists,
but not those
Who through Spirit and Beauty,
ennoble their art.

XXVI

Petrarch, it seems, loved his art more
Than his beloved, for with his poetry
He wished to build a lasting monument to love.

More than the to-and-fro of the censers,
The saint Tiruválluvar loved to look longingly
At the temple from afar, which
As a pariah he did not have the right to enter.

Laura, symbol of love. The temple wall,
Symbol of priestly religion.
We can love God's grace in our heart
More than the symbol, for it comes from Within.

XXVII

Asceticism purifies, and so does the Ganges' water —
But nothing purifies like knowledge,
Say the wise. For nothing else can so clearly
Testify to the True, and vanquish illusion.

XXVIII

Ātmā and *Māyā* — everything is said
In this exposition of the Highest Light;
What is, is, and cannot be otherwise.

Ātmā is the In-Itself, for Itself alone —
Ātmā is also the origin of all primordial powers;
Māyā is *Ātmā*'s ray; all else is nothing.

XXIX

Not only renunciation, not only knowledge,
But also beauty, if one understands it aright,
Is a purification — if the gaze of our spirit
Penetrates appearances and reaches the inward.

XXX

He who observes that another is a fool
Is not obliged to be a fool himself,
Out of some false notion of justice; one should
Not confuse objective thinking with self-praise.

XXXI

So many people walk on false paths
And blindly hope that God will give them grace.
One should look honestly in the mirror of Truth,
And unsparingly take oneself in hand.

XXXII

One would like to know, who is "I am,"
Because it makes us sad to feel that our "I" is nothing.
Be still — thou wilt find thy soul's repose
If, instead of "I am," thou keepest Pure Being in mind.

XXXIII

Who art thou to criticize Protagoras?
Someone could have asked of Plato;
If Plato had then said: I am Plato,
People would have laughed — they did not want to recognize him.
Plato — and also Dante — knew who they were,
Just as generations after them did.

XXXIV

Man must not presumptuously expect grace;
There is no place for blind pride in God's garden.
If thou lookest calmly in the mirror of Truth,
The bolts of Heaven's doors will open for thee.

XXXV

Thou shouldst plant the Good in thy soul
By ceaseless repetition of the Remembrance
And experience of things that liberate —
Of self-illumination and self-giving.

XXXVI

Of course thou must think of earthly things,
Thou canst not do otherwise; but every day
The stuff of thinking must be swept away,
When the Peace of God lays itself over thy heart.

Some things are beautiful, but many make one tired;
The world is agitation – but God is Peace, Peace.

XXXVII

Krishna, in his human form,
Took part in the battle of Kurukshetra;
But suddenly, in the presence of Sanjaya, he showed
His divinity, powerful, radiating and overwhelming.
Thus does the Divine Nature wish to dwell within man;
It wishes to be enthroned in his heart as it is in Heaven –

In every man lies his Way to salvation.

XXXVIII

On the one hand, the world is transience;
On the other, it is that which is: content as such.
Earthly experiences must pass away –
But the God-willed form is beyond all time,
Because it bespeaks the true Substance;
What is Divine in nature cannot disappear.

The Lord is absolute, existence is relative –
A half being. God is infinity –
Hence the starry-heaven of forms –
Hence the mystery of differentiation.

XXXIX

Is not the individual absolute in his own way?
Certainly; but the multiplicity of I-consciousness
Is contradictory; how so?
Because everyone, just like thyself, wears the garment of egoity.

The One Self sows its profound Being
In the God-willed space of the finite.

XL

Every soul is an astrological-alchemical
Symbol; this means
That man will either squander his salvation,
Or, by God's light and grace,
Attain the meaning of earthly life.

Be not concerned about the origin of this symbol —
Thou wast hidden within All-Possibility.

XLI

Man lives in the outward, motley world,
Confronted by things both great and small.
God-consciousness flows towards the deep Center —
In the inward thou wilt find love's peace.

XLII

Nothing can chain us to earthly dreams —
For, like a ship, our way goes forward
Upon great waves — by an invisible Hand
Drawn firmly through the foam of this world.

XLIII

God-consciousness means removing oneself
From *Māyā*'s play of worldly thoughts,
And then a perpetual affirmation of That
Which is the goal of thy God-willed existence;
It is peace and joy in That which liberates,
And whose deepest being is beatitude;
Knowing that this One alone is real,
And that thou art not other than *Ātmā*.

XLIV

Ātmā alone: this is the fundamental concept.
Ātmā and *Māyā*: it is good that thou shouldst know this.
Māyā in *Ātmā*: this is creative Being;
Ātmā in *Māyā* is thine own spirit.

XLV

Three human types: first the one who wants only to enjoy;
Next the ascetic, stubborn despiser of the world;
And then the guardian of a wise equilibrium.
The latter two can be saints,
But not the worldly man, who seeks only enjoyment.

The fool does not understand the meaning of pleasure;
The ascetic is one who sees through the world
But mistrusts his own nature.
Be thou conscious of the Divine content of all
That God's grace has vouchsafed to thee.

XLVI

Morning, midday, evening, night –
Thus has the Lord made time.
Day followed by night: after activity,
Respose in contemplativity.

Spring, summer, autumn and winter –
Life's spaces within time;
Childhood, youth, maturity, old age –
Open thyself, O eternity!

XLVII

Autumn – it slips downwards into the snow
And flees; one could expect nothing else
After all the tired leaves swept away by the wind.
But that spring should come – this is the miracle;
The garden will bloom like a gift from heaven.

Thus it is with the soul that discovers God –
When after all the hardships of the world,
God's grace awakens it to His light.

XLVIII

On the day that my oldest friend passed away,
I received his last letter.
I have known this loyal friend since our schooldays;
It is difficult to believe that he no longer is.
At his grave, in order to do something meaningful,
Someone read four of my didactic poems.
An old proverb says: the beginning and the end –
By God's will – clasp hands.

XLIX

Our Intellect must emphasize different things
Depending on the moment; such is life.
Many doors open towards God;
So there must be more than one key –

Ways of feeling or of understanding.
Let the high powers of Heaven weave
The wondrous work of our spiritual garment.

L

"Say: God, then leave them to their idle chatter" –
So says the Koran. A *hadīth* of the Messenger:
"Believers are always in a good state" –
A saying that holy men know in their hearts.
"Is it not in the remembrance of God
That hearts find rest?"
"In the presence of God, there is no idle talk –
Only Peace, Peace is worthy of speech."

LI

One should call a thing by the right name:
What astonishes me is the incapacity of so many people
To think, who think in an irresponsible way:
Be great, and thou wilt have a free hand in small things.
In reality, greatness manifests itself
In this: that even little things are right and perfect.
What destroys the power of reflection
Is prejudice and passion.

LII

Earth, water, air and fire
Are contained deeply within ether;
At the same time, they are forms
That unfold ether's inner content.

The elements – primordial powers
That radiate from the Divine Nature;
In thine own soul too
Thou canst find traces of them.

And in the Intellect that guides thee –
And gives thee, by the grace of God,
The wondrous gifts of Primordial Being.

LIII

We knew a group of young girl dancers
From the distant island of Bali;
One of them showed me a little book,
And wanted me to sign my name in it.
Magical beauty, moving temperament,
Such as bloom in the south-sea paradise;
Ye lotus blossoms from a far and blessèd land –
From you, the soul can learn;
Be it only that, amongst other gifts,
We have a sense of the All-Powerful's smile.

LIV

Snowflakes – crystals silently floating down
From heaven: enchanting formations,
That lay themselves slowly on earth's face –
Like a cool, white veil, tender and mild.

Crystals – like different forms
Of spirit and faith; for the One,
Born of God, wishes to unfold
Inward Infinity toward the outward.

LV

Justice – a wonderful word,
Full of truth and consolation; it is the judgment
After all wrongs. Let the demon rage –
Victory goes to God-willed equilibrium.

Justice in feeling and in thinking –
You should direct all that you are towards the Truth.

LVI

Amongst the *Avatāras*, there is a type
That does not bring a spiritual message of peace,
But rather pertains to the world: Alexander,
Through whose sword the Greek kingdom awoke;
And Caesar, called divine – the hand of destiny.
So that a Divine plan might unfold,
And turn much misfortune to something better.

LVII

The Lorelei who sang high up on a cliff;
A fairy tale that has resounded since olden times.
Whoever looked on her was doomed to destruction –
He had to die in the waves of the Rhine.

A martyr – it is said in Islam –
Is the man whose heart is broken by love;
Whoever must die from love's deep wounds –
The All-Merciful rejects him not.

Blessèd is he who dies the death of the spirit,
And earns the life of Eternity.
Far be it that wisdom should lose hope –
God-remembrance knows no complaint.

"Blessèd are they that mourn on earth,
For they shall be comforted."

LVIII

"Whoso knoweth his soul,
Also knoweth his Lord."
"Love thy neighbor as thyself" –
This is the kernel of the message.

Two sayings, from two Messengers of God –
Not everyone has understood them.
The I of the neighbor is my own I:
The Self of the Most High is Being in Itself.

LIX

The *Christos Pantokrator* is an image
That ought not to exist in sacred art.
"Not made by human hand"?
One wonders what the artist meant.

This image is a testimony to sentiment and piety —
But not to the man Jesus. It seeks to show
The human god; but in reality
One should keep silent before the mystery of Christ.

LX

Shri Shankara and Shri Abhinavagupta:
Vedanta and Tantra. Both are paths
To salvation — one to the right, the other to the left,
But the two unite on Heaven's shore,
Ending in the same grace of God.
Here, renunciation — there, contemplative experience:
To interiorize what the world's images offer.

LXI

Thou wast born a human being;
No better thing can a creature be.
Thou hast found the path to God,
The best of all possible gifts.
So it should not trouble thee
If dark powers rage at thee;
Thou knowest what thou wantest — *Deo gratias* —
So let them think what they will.

LXII

The night has come — it has gently woven itself around thee
With a song that sings of love;
Be grateful, for consolation comes from Above,
For Rādhā, with golden breasts and loving arms,
Brings thee a greeting from Heaven —
A greeting of Goodness and Mercy.
Access to God thou hast at every moment;
Angels too bring thee tidings from the Most High.

LXIII

Krishna is Vishnu, god of becoming and life;
Rādhā is Lakshmī, goddess of love and happiness.
The *Avatāras* bring to earth
What otherwise would remain hidden in the Divine —

Mystery of the exteriorization of the Good;
God too must live in the flood of *Māyā*.

LXIV

Contentment, then trust — ask not
In what life's wayfarer should trust.
Trust as such: faith in salvation
Is to look upon the faraway ideal with God-willed resignation —
No "where" and "how." The All-Merciful will
Build for the soul the final bridge.

LXV

The night came with its magic flute,
And Leila sang her love song from afar
Throughout my dream until the blush of dawn,
While the veil of darkness parted from us.

Then came the day and brought its woes,
But also remembrance of essential things —
Above all, after the dream's sweetness and solace,
The radiance of Wisdom, reminding and awakening.

There was the solace and music of beauty—
And then the luminous bliss of the pure Spirit.

LXVI

"O God, let us see things
As they really are" — a saying of God's Messenger.
Therein lies the quintessence of all wisdom —
The principle which thinkers, imprisoned in their prejudices,
Have often failed to appreciate.

The kernel of Truth is as old as the world.

LXVII

About compassion thou shouldst have no doubts;
Thou knowest the parable of the prodigal son.
Whoever, after erring, finds his center,
The Most High gives him all the more beautiful a reward.

Hold fast to God and let the world turn —
Then thou wilt find thy soul in the One.

LXVIII

The everyday state of the soul fluctuates,
Even if we do not suffer from a vice.
It is not easy to remain at the center;
Many things make a mockery of us —
Of the outer soul, but not its inner kernel,

Which is a rock when it gives itself to the Lord.

LXIX

Thou shouldst not strive to understand a problem,
When thou well knowest that God understands it,
And that, whatever be thy difficulty,
Pain disappears in a believing heart.

Hold fast to what is certitude for thee,
And be confident. The rest is indifferent.

LXX

It has often been said that it is a grave mistake
Not to listen to both sides —
And, in spite of manifest reality,
To swear by one's own false opinion;

One-sidedness brings vain deceit and pain.
The sister of Truth is Justice —
Truth is worth more than any treasures in the world.

LXXI

If something causes pain, man should always think
That he should have been grateful before,
When nothing afflicted him –
Grateful for the grace of living without pain.

Consider well: patience and resignation
Are intimately bound up with gratitude.

LXXII

Holy water and holy incense –
Purification and a striving upwards;
Water and fire. Firstly the death of illusion –
And then new birth in eternal life.

LXXIII

Remembrance of the One Reality
Dispels what is merely dream and froth,
For invincible is the Act of the Spirit,
The Remembrance of God; and illusion vanishes.

The Act of the Spirit – in it God is content
As well as agent. Whereas thou, O man,
Art merely bearer of His Being and His Willing.

LXXIV

In peace resides happiness; hast thou ever seen it here below?
Perfect peace thou findest in God alone.
So seek thy peace in the Peace of the Godhead;
In the Eternal – and thou wilt be in bliss.

LXXV

Dream-cities and dream-streets of my wanderings,
City paradises — all this is past.
Destiny brought me to a vast forest —
Its deep silence is dearer to my heart.

LXXVI

Serenity is like the pure air
Of a mountain peak close to Heaven;
Certitude is the fragrance of the deep earth —
The happiness of the immutable center, where I stand.

Resignation is the peace of my soul,
For what is written, let it come to pass;
Trust is to move towards a goal —
Going forward in the happiness of hope.

LXXVII

Mohammed said: haste comes from the devil,
But slowness is pleasing to the Lord.
The bad person is always in flight from himself;
The good person walks like the evening star.

Haste may be useful; but slowness bears
God's peace, which descends upon the heart.

LXXVIII

Prudence is needful. *Quidquid agis, prudenter agas;*
Respice finem – constantly.

Festina lente. Be not like the grass
That every wind blows back and forth.

Whatever thou doest, do it with prudence;
And from the beginning, think of the result.

Hasten slowly – the one who rushes
Knows not what blessing lies in tranquility.

LXXIX

Be surprised at nothing – *nihil mirari;*
So said Horace. For what is, cannot not be,
Whether we understand it or not.
If we commit it to God, our thinking is pure.

LXXX

Carpe diem does not mean that life is enjoyment –
It means that happiness can only come from moderation;
Whatever is governed by moderation is interiorizing;
Only in what is noble wilt thou experience God's open hand.

LXXXI

A special kind of beauty is dignity:
He who understands and loves it participates in the One
Within life's stream; nobility of comportment
Is to unite the human state with the Being of God —

Participation in the Center, that never wavers,
Is God-remembrance, grateful for existence.

LXXXII

I live now, in this instant —
And in no other;
With all the creatures and things which journey
Through the universe with me.

What for me is now, is now for others too,
Great and small;
There are no exceptions, none at all,
In the powerful stream of time.

Each moment that flies from me
Is history;
Each moment ceaselessly destroys the now
That went before it.

God grant that I find peace
In the eternal Now;
And discover in my heart
The meaning of all we are.

LXXXIII

For the Lord of the worlds, millennia are
As a flash of lightning, an instant;
He sees what happens in His "Now," —
All is one, He does not look back.

Thou may'st be bewildered by space and time,
Thy feeble thinking cannot fathom them —
Thou must leave the mystery of infinity
To the Creator of the universe.

LXXXIV

Learned philosophers have disputed much
About questions of space and time;
It is strange that one has endured so much hair-splitting
About something that everyone can see for himself.

Space is nothing other than expansion;
And, if nothing fills it, it is the emptiness of ether.
It is senseless that the flow of time —
Which can not exist when nothing happens —
Should trouble the head of him who seeks the In-Itself.

LXXXV

Unicity is irresistible —
The whole world could be crushed by It.
May the true One-and Only, which shines divinely —
Illumine the dark night of illusion.
Relative being is shattered against the wall of Pure Being —
What is not the Great One, is nothing.

Nevertheless: the relative, through grace,
May become Unity, on the best of all paths.

LXXXVI

Serenity — it is unconditional,
And so is resignation to God's Will.
Certitude — it is evident in itself;
May it fill thy soul with trust in God.
I have said it before in different words;
Meet thyself thus wherever thou art.

LXXXVII

Interiorization is the great word
For the one who has not chosen renunciation of the world:
It is not pleasures that give meaning to life,
But moderation, which steels the will
And leads back to the Inward.
Either leave beauty to itself,
Or else gaze deeply into it —
There where dwells the One—there where I am

LXXXVIII

Music from time to time; for music cannot be
The "always" of the soul — let the soul be silent in God.
For if thou desirest God's presence,
Thou too must show Him thy heart and thy soul.

LXXXIX

Destiny wills that thou walk on highest peaks;
And so it may happen that thou wonderest:
Where is the homeland that my heart dreams of —
And thou complainest to the Most High.

But what thou art, thou must be it and live it;
And what thou bringest, it must be brought to the world.
Man must be resigned to the Path and to Duty —
After the night God lets the morning dawn.

XC

To lie down, ruminate, and dream,
Is not rest. Thoughts can always
Wander far and wide; thou findest peace
In God alone; what His nearness gives thee —
Thou wilt never find in worldly tumult.

XCI

Religion seeks to speak to everyone;
For it, the interest of society takes precedence,
As does the salvation of even the least of men;
Religion saves from the misery of original sin.

Metaphysics looks at the nature of things,
Without opposing the formalism of religion;
Think not that it too is dogma and morals —
It sees much more than do the religious forms.

XCII

Spiritual truths are beauties that enlighten;
If thou hast understood the true,
It will give thee joy. Likewise,
The ship of beauty will reach the port of truth –
Every light has its melody.

XCIII

Each virtue is a beautiful woman,
And so is every profound truth;
Whoever loves not truth and virtue,
Is like a man who is asleep in the sun.

To love the true and the good means:
To live with them and to kindle their light;
To cause one's own soul to awake in them –
Through them, to find the way to the God of love.

XCIV

To stand before God with a spiritual act that affirms Him,
That shapes the soul and gives rise to hope.
To stand before Him with a silence
That removes all egoism from the soul.

To stand before God—and to wish for nothing else;
To take joy in His Compassion.
He alone is the One, the All-Highest;
And He dwells in thee—now and in eternity.

XCV

Fasting is purification. He who cannot fast
Should fast in his soul. For the man who has been
Given much by Heaven should give back to the
One Creator something of his life.

XCVI

Chance does not exist; and yet there is
Something that one could call chance;
One should distinguish what has an incidental existence
From what has a definite meaning.

Nonetheless, both are relative.
Not so the distinction between God and the world:
Between the One that cannot not be,
And things which are, because it pleases the Lord.

XCVII

"They that are whole do not need a physician,"
Said Jesus; he came to deliver from sin
Only those who had gone astray;
And them he took unto himself.

His saying has also a broader meaning:
Because he who is born for Wisdom
Carries a message in the depths of his heart —
And the words of this message are not lost.

XCVIII

Do not say to the world: How canst thou console me?
Come, help me, give me happiness.
Say rather to the world: I stand before my Lord;
He is the One. And I console thee.

XCIX

Beware of miserable pettiness;
Justice is what becomes the noble man –
And generosity. See how, for the fool, it may happen
That for a small thing, he goes to hell.
I would by no means call hell eternal –
But the flames of purgatory also burn.
Many people who thought they were great,
Were pushed by devils into the furnace.

On the other hand, someone can go to Heaven
For a very small act,
And God forgives him far graver things –
Therefore, O man, be careful over small things!
There was a woman, who, from a far-off fountain,
Brought water to a thirsty dog,
And God – because of her goodness and patience –
Forgave her all her sins.

C

There is Pure Being, which is Unity;
Then there are the things that constitute existence;
Serenity is to feel and think on the level of Pure Being;
It is to watch over the soul,
And not to be sick from a poison. Cast out the poison,
And with it, all triviality and all sin.

Look at the snow, it has no desires –
It lays its veil over all things.

CI

The eagle and the owl – two birds
That are sacred to peoples far and wide.
The first means: loftiness and sharp discernment,
The second: profundity and contemplation.
The first rules by day, the second by night;
Rich is the symbolism that the Lord has made.

CII

The rose and the water-lily –
The latter contemplative, the former glowing with love;
Both created for man's soul;
And each one blooming before the Face of God.

CIII

Many years ago, by the pyramids,
I rode on a high dromedary,
Over golden sands, in the southern heat –
And I no longer knew where I had been born.
The day was unusually beautiful.
Why should I not put this into words?
I have mentioned so many other images,
I also wanted to let this one speak.

Days, like millennia, pass away –
The desert wind scatters them in the sand.

CIV

I have often been on the wide sea —
In other words: the sea has often been with me.
For the sea came into my destiny:
An image of Pure Being — a wondrous We.

An image of the Spirit that experiences Pure Being,
And reposes in the essence of things, beyond all time;
Consciousness of Him who is because He is —
Experience of drunken Infinity.

CV

Ātmā and *Māyā* — a divine pair;
Purusha and *Prákriti*: primordial Idea
And primordial matter. Likewise Spirit and soul —
Everywhere these two, wherever I look,
Ready for love and manifestation.

Within the One, duality is deeply contained;
The One wills to unfold its All in a pair —
The limitlessness of the Absolute.

CVI

The tree of the soul: the root is the heart,
The trunk is the personality,
And each of the branches — in principle four —
Symbolizes a faculty of the Spirit:
Reason, sentiment, imagination and memory —
Outwardly, and inwardly still deeper.
The blossoms are our intentions, and the fruits
Are our deeds — in the light of Truth.

CVII

Contentment – be happy with the Path
That God has given thee,
And wish not for thyself another life
On the path of thy destiny.
Think not of a far-off time
That was more beautiful;
For what thou livest now, in contentment,
Is wonderful.

CVIII

The crows take flight –
Their shrill tones pierce the forest;
Autumn leaves spiral down –
O, time of white peace, come soon.

Such is the soul –
When the turmoil of the world disturbs its silence;
When no Grace
Defends it from restless thought.

May the quiet of purity
Pervade the space of our thinking;
In God's nearness –
The world may be the world, but you scarcely hear it.

CIX

There are three substances in every human being:
The first one is what makes him human;
The second makes the individual man –
The third is what the individual's spirit has engendered.

Thou has responsibility for what thou art –
But God created what makes the human state.

CX

One can experience the God-willed beauty of this world
As a sinner, a slave of passion—
Or as a wise man, who penetrates
What God's love and compassion create.

The penitent has the right to repent of his weakness—
But God has the right to sweeten the struggle for the strong.

CXI

Pope Pius XII worked himself to death,
Because he thought that work was virtue —
For him, the accomplishment of duty was sanctity,
The pious "thou must," whose goal is the Most High.

Far more essential for a pontiff
Is contemplation. A priest may well have duties
To the outside world — but he should above all,
Motionless before God, accomplish the inner vision.

This the holy pope did, many will say.
I say yes and no — as to his place in Heaven,
No believing soul should ask.

CXII

Abraham Lincoln believed in the people,
Because he did not know how people are;
He believed that the majority were like himself,
Noble and pious — children of the same spirit.
The good man often confuses the ideal
With the appearance thereof — with the mere husk;
Not because he presumes to say wise words,
But out of humility, he wishes to believe the good.

CXIII

The good man longs for heavenly bliss —
Only he has a sense of the vision of God and of peace;
Most people feel happy
In the agitation that they themselves are here below.
But he who would attain what God offers us,
Must within himself resemble Heaven.
That someone has a sense of silence in God
Does not prevent him from fulfilling
His earthly duty conscientiously and with gratitude.

CXIV

The Truth of God is the Absolute,
And absolute should be the Joy
That rings out from the True;
To piety and wisdom's grace
Both Truth and Joy belong. Be thou a reflection
Of what radiates from Pure Being.

CXV

The name of man — a possibility.
The Name of God — Being, Spirit, Power,
And Felicity, from out of which shines Beauty,
And the Compassion that watches over the world.

Be thou with Him, and He will be with thee;
And if thou callest His Name, He will enter into thee,
For He has put Himself into His Word.

Powerful is His Name within time,
And mighty the majesty of His holiness.

CXVI

Sadness is a kind of unconscious revolt,
A lack of resignation and trust;
One who, without resistance, lets himself be seduced
By the soul's moods, lacks trust in the All-Merciful.

The root of every noble tendency is
Trust in God — the meaning of earthly life.

CXVII

What is not nothing, must be the All;
Nothing does not exist, so there is only Being.
If there were no Being, things would not exist;
We living beings live on the razor's edge of existence.

And, if thou canst think, thou knowest that God was there
Before all things, before all living beings.
It is God who saw thee in Himself eternally;
Before thine earthly existence — thy spirit was there.

CXVIII

Say not that the wise man should not love beauty;
The ascetic cannot change the nature of things.
Think not that beauty is a mere trifle and pastime;
Beauty is the wife of Divine Truth.

Whatever is beautiful, O Creator, belongs to Thee;
Because beauty is the True — it is Pure Being.

CXIX

Earthly life is an inn, and the innkeeper
Is God, who has prepared everything for the meal;
Everyone has his duty; and the Lord of life
Is waiting for life's guest to pay.
If thou, O man, would'st obtain God's favor,
Be logical – and pay thy debt.

CXX

That thou remainest in peace, thou owest to God,
Even if the wickedness of the foolish threatens thee;
For God is always God, and thy soul
Has access to the Lord in all distress.

Thy soul is what it has chosen;
Be happy if a trial of this world –
Woven of illusion, but sent by God –
Makes thee better, and strengthens thy will.

Be what thou art, though the sea run dry –
The last word belongs to the Lord of the worlds.

CXXI

In my father's time: "Hear, O people, what I say:
The clock in the belfry has struck twelve;
And twelve, O people, is the number of the apostles."
Something similar was faithfully sung
Throughout the night, at every hour,
As our night-watchman made his round.

And thus it sounds in the soul of man –
As if his spiritual consciousness counted
His faithful meetings with the Lord –
Heartbeat after heartbeat, like star upon star.
It is in the nature of the wise man's spirit,
To remember his sacred duty hour by hour.

CXXII

The Inward and the Outward: this means
The Truth, and then the Beauty of this world;
The First and the Last: certitude
Which deeply contains the peace of our soul;
Truth and beauty, security and peace —
In God, and in our soul here below.

CXXIII

"Though this be madness, yet there's method in it" —
Said Shakespeare. Clever madness has become the fashion —
There are more and more mentally deranged people:
This comes from the accursed emphasis on the ego
That prevails everywhere today —
Too many souls are the dwelling-place of the devil.
Each thinks he is the adornment of humanity,
Instead of understanding:
Truth is more than we.

CXXIV

Beauty, as also mental acuity, are a loan;
Only what we do for the Lord has merit.
One can squander the gifts of nature,
But whether we be strong or weak,
Let us repose in the Most High.

What nature has loaned us must be sanctified;
He who appreciates it, walks in the tracks of God.

CXXV

In old age, one begins to falter —
And to suffer from this or that woe;
It seems that the body is no longer really thine —
So may the Lord be thy health.

CXXVI

Life is not a closed house; thou, O believer,
Livest not only in the here-below.
"Where thy treasure is, there will thy heart be also."
The wise and the pious also live in the hereafter.

CXXVII

In the spirit of man there is a kernel,
And it is infallible. In the language of Jesus,
This is the Holy Ghost. It cannot be forgiven if,
Out of passion, thou deniest what thou knowest.

CXXVIII

Truth manifests itself: sometimes as form
In a particular faith; sometimes as the primordial content
Of a knowledge, whose profound essence
Depends on neither condition nor form.

Whatever thou receivest through God's will —
Be it a formal faith or an inner light —
Is the Holy Spirit; to resist it
Out of obstinacy, the Most High will not forgive.

The Lord does not ask more than thou canst give —
But what thou canst give is for thee an absolute duty.

CXXIX

The doctrine of merit is to be found
In the parable of the entrusted talents.

Thou canst not give the Lord, or thyself, anything better
Than, deep within the nothing, to think of the All.

It is a sin not to fulfill
What the angels do when they sing of the Most High.

CXXX

Stillness of mind — it has as a corollary
The affirmation of God — so be ready for the Word.

Contentment — it can build a castle for thee;
Following it comes fervor — a warm trust in God.

Discernment between God and the world —
And then the Selfhood, that contains thyself.

CXXXI

Thou who art All — Thou dwellest in the sound
Of the Name, Presence of the Highest Truth;
The portrait of Thy nature is my consolation —
The Light of the Spirit together with Thy Being.

Truth and Presence. Divine doctrine
Is the uncreated Word of the All-One.
Presence — the meeting with the Lord —
Is, in the world and in ourselves, the Highest Place.

CXXXII

Stories, plays, and fables –
so some scholars say –
Should be understood symbolically,
and this should be explanation enough;
Nevertheless: what stories tell us
must have a meaning on its own plane,
Otherwise symbolic interpretation
is but jest and shimmering deceit.
One can never excuse stupid puzzles
by spiritual interpretation;
Give us beauty and truth,
not wild yarns and lies.
In fact the purpose of tragedy,
as Aristotle said, is catharsis;
Offered only chaotic action,
the seeker after Wisdom will find nothing.
Mytho-poetical tale-spinning
is a common human weakness –
The wise man, *Deo juvante,*
would rather reflect on the nature of things

CXXXIII

Two things are of the essence: God and my spirit;
God, the root of all Being; and my spirit, which is
Conscious of Him who is All.

The He of the Creator, and the created I.

CXXXIV

In old age, one is more world-aware
Than in youth. For one understands
Not only that this and that happened,
But also how the wheel of destiny turns.

Youth sees the content, image after image —
But not whence or whither the world-wind blows.
In youth, one can imagine, but not experience,
The "how" of the world-web.

The "so" of things, one can already see as a child —
The enigmatic "how" reveals itself only later.

CXXXV

Two things make man happy
Within the framework of life's loan:
Firstly the beautiful, which he has the right to experience;
And then his creative activity, whose meaning gives him joy.

Above this shines, like the star of benediction,
The happiness of everything that brings us to the Lord.

CXXXVI

Father Julien Aymard always wished
To contemplate the sacred monstrance;
This was given to him; it was his spiritual way,
His paradise in the world here below —
Like the pariah Tiruválluvar,
Who wished to contemplate the temple roof from afar.

For there are saints who have the grace
Of building for themselves a way to Paradise
From outward things that manifest the Inward.

CXXXVII

The Curé d'Ars, people say, was not intelligent;
A superficial judgment, for, with a saint,
Mere thinking counts for little, because his heart —
By the grace of God — can bestow Heaven itself.

The little child says: "I am small, my heart is pure" —
For adults too, this must be possible.

CXXXVIII

In one of his hymns, Shankara says:
Even if thou performest miracles, what will this profit thee?
Floating in the air will not help thee
In thy liberation from *samsāra*.

And this he often repeated.
Why? Not to teach the reader —
But because his joy over
What Brahma had given him, urged him
To honor it through a profusion of words.

CXXXIX

The voice of man is in itself a prayer;
Yet even animals do not wish to be without prayer.
God gives them a spark of piety —
Animals pray without knowing it.

So animals' sounds are not mere cries —
God put something of Himself into them;
The creatures pray in the way they must.

Man's call to God seeks to reveal
What all voices were before creation.

CXL

The spiritual message is multiform,
And one must understand it in all of its forms:
First, there is Truth, which becomes doctrine;
With it the striving towards the heights of Truth.
Then the message of the Master's personality,
Which brings a special blessing.
Then, in the world, there is God-given beauty,
In which the splendor of the Divine resounds.

CXLI

Esoterism is firstly a path
Within a religious form; it is religion at a deeper level.
But then it transcends all forms,
It is more than a reward for religious virtue.
Assuredly the revealed form is true,
But Truth is not a narrow form;
For Pure Truth can only be one.

The nature of things is the Spirit's norm.

CXLII

The destiny that forms us — this is one thing;
We live it from day to day.
I-consciousness is the tapestry of our soul —
Image of the long dream through which we wander.

And yet we are more than this picture:
God has given Himself to us in our sou;
Far beyond the things we encounter,
The eternal life of the spirit shines like a star.

Songs without Names

Ninth Collection

Prayer — the highest truth resounds
In thee, within thy deepest core.
Had the whole world forgotten thee,
The All-Merciful would remember thee.
If the soul will turn to God,
So that He help it carry its burden,
God will take a hundred steps to meet it.

Songs without Names

Ninth Collection

I

The contents of thy consciousness thou must choose;
Do not be dominated by images.
Think of That which is greater than all things –
May Eternity take possession of thy being.

II

Thou shouldst not fear the emptiness of God –
Know that, in its way, the world is
Emptiness; so let God fill it –
And watch over thy heart with His Presence.

If God seems empty to thee, it is only because
Thou hast not found thy peace in Him.

III

The saint, the hero, the genius:
Three summits in the world of man;
Each on its own, or all three in one –
A genius, who is a saint and a hero.

A genius can be either good or worldly,
And likewise the hero.
                    Linked to God
And blissful, is the saint alone.

IV

Genius and saint and hero; but what of the sage?
In true wisdom there is also sanctity.
On the other hand, not every saint is ready
For the lofty path of knowledge.

God knows best where the soul stands,
And where and how the wind of the Spirit blows.

V

There are mystics who, without any act of the will,
Receive Heaven's nourishment through grace;
And there are others, in whom spirit and will
Combine, in order to reach the Light.

Ecstasy, given by grace, is one thing;
Another is gnosis, which dwells in the heart —
The power of the Most High and the kernel of bliss.

VI

There are people, but they are rare, whose spirit,
From birth — along with other gifts —
Loves the essential; and therefore
They have no home here on earth.

VII

There are fortunate people who even as children,
Though much beleagured — tend towards the One;
And who from the very beginning, without knowing it,
Are in God's loving hands.

VIII

Something that is not easy to understand
Is why humanity should think
That everything in the world is in order,
Despite the fact that what logically is one, appears as many.

Do not remain trapped in this naïve illusion;
Ye should know that Selfhood by definition is unique.
The enigma of enigmas is that this One
Becomes many. There is no other enigma.

IX

Strange how he who has joy in the Greatest,
Also finds pleasure in the smallest of things;
This is because the spirit that enters the Inward
Unites the soul with Joy as such;
And because the sage — by the Light of the Greatest —
Can speak the latter's language also with the smallest.

X

The *jivan-mukta* — according to Shankara —
Is free from the world, even if he talks with a child
Or a beautiful woman —
He is free from foolishness and sin.

He too is touched by pleasure and pain here below —
But his inner reality is free from both.
It is also said, that in the misery of this earth
His nature shines, so that morning will come.

XI

Above: means That which is unique;
Deep down: That which thou art through the One.
In front: what thou graspest in deep hope;
Behind: what thou abandonest on thy Path.
Right: what I do to manifest the Most High;
Left: that I find my peace in God.

XII

It is said that God dwells in the highest Heaven:
This means that honor is due to Him alone;
That He, the Lord, is on His throne above all creation —
For, compared with Him, even Heaven is emptiness.

God also dwells within creation, so to speak;
Otherwise it would collapse into nothingness.
He also dwells in the heart of those who are wise —
The wind of the Spirit blows where God wills.

XIII

Deep beneath the water sleeps an old castle
Because, a thousand years ago,
A city sank into the sea; because a sinful people
Drowned overnight in the cold flood.

So it is related in Vineta's legend.
It is a symbol of what can happen
When a soul forgets the sacred,
And is swallowed up by Divine Wrath.

The sacred: that which manifests the Lord;
Wrath: the darksome ground of self-deception.
The souls of Vineta may be in Heaven —
Ye know not whom the Most High forgives.

XIV

People who have a narrow faith
Respect only what they believe;
If the wind of truth blows too high,
The fox looks at sour grapes.

Other people are blind to faith,
They respect only the screws of the mind;
Any child is in a better state –
But one cannot preach to the deaf.

XV

One must sometimes speak of unpleasant things;
What has to be said, must be said,
For the world is made of a to-and-fro.
One's duty done, consolation can once more resound.

Injustice is also written in the stars;
Be not discouraged – thou couldst learn some good from it.

XVI

Lallā was naked, because she had found the Self.
The peoples's astonishment could not hurt her;
For her charms – which did not fear the light –
Were her sermon for the people.

She wanted to rejoice in the Inward;
What she gave to her surroundings was her being.
The wind's caresses were to her a reminder
Of highest Truth – and deepest Inwardness.

XVII

The Name of God is the sound of thunder –
Yet it is also silence, deepest stillness.
It is the Creator's limitless power –
But it is beyond all existential fullness.

Two things must be within thee: the strength of the Spirit –
And with it non-existence, beyond all works.

XVIII

"There is no god but the one God."
"The remembrance of God is the greatest of things."
Thus it is said in the Koran; and therein all has been said –
It only remains for thee to give thyself to the Lord.

XIX

The skeptic asks: why do ye believe in God?
We do not wish to plow through this theologically;
For what soul and spirit have understood –
Gives us life, and gives you the lie.

XX

Juice becomes wine; thus is it willed by nature.
In Islam, drinking wine is forbidden;
When wine results, hath not God willed it thus?
Let not man's weakness be blamed.

Shaikh Mulay 'Alī had a brother
In the mountains who pressed juice from grapes;
It seemed to the Shaikh that it was rather wine –
His brother said: God knows, and does, what is best.

XXI

The noble fool – a strange possibility;
Cervantes described it in a masterly way.
Don Quixote did not lack wisdom –
But he pushed his madness rather far.

When he – the author – invented characters,
To whom exaggeration permitted every jest,
He did so to express what he himself thought,
But did not dare to say.

XXII

The *Kumbha Mela* is a Hindu festival
At which thousands of pilgrims meet;
From every sect, and every part of India,
From north to south, and east to west.

The water of the Ganges purifies from sins –
And so does the vision of naked *sadhus*
Thronging through the place. By gazing on their holy bodies,
Every soul can find a part of its salvation.

But the all-too-human is not absent: all along
The sects have often had bloody disputes;
Thereby straying far from the purpose of the thing –
And much further still from holiness.

XXIII

The purely outward is dark space;
The purely inward is luminous spirit.
Space is boundless, spirit is center;
Between the two is what one calls the universe.

Within space there are spheres, constantly in motion,
With light and warmth; suns and their rays;
Also planets. Life and consciousness are
The containers of the Spirit linked to God.

XXIV

Space: limitless Being that contains everything.
Sphere: existence, form, perfection.
Light: the Spirit which is our illumination;
Warmth: love, goodness, bliss.

XXV

Let worldly things come to thee as they will.
Think not in advance how things should be for thee —
Does not every hour have its own care or happiness?
If only the One be thine!

XXVI

Transcience and imperfection —
The latter in space and the former in time.
Yet, in the space-time of the world, thou findest
Traces of the Divine — traces of Eternity.

XXVII

Firstly: what is ephemeral has already passed away.
Secondly: thou hast always been an earthly creature
With shortcomings; woven into the workings of the world.
Only the Spirit is free.

XXVIII

Adiáphora – what canst thou do if the world
Persecutes thee with things that are but trifles?
They run through thy thoughts and seek
To dominate thee and disturb thy peace in the Spirit.
On the one hand, thou must be resigned;
On the other, thou must strive towards liberation –
Knowing full well that straw and dust are part of life.

XXIX

The Lord is stern; but He is also mild,
Depending on how man behaves on the path;
Every wayfarer – for "the flesh is weak" –
Needs the rod and also care.
Be not astonished when God's trial comes –
Nor when God beautifies thy path.

XXX

The Name of God is like a ship,
In which the soul sails to the further shore.
See how the weak swimmer can defend himself
Only with difficulty against the wild waves' assault,
And only with effort can reach Heaven's shore.

With God's help the difficult becomes easy.

XXXI

Apart from purely profane science,
There is only one thing: child-like experience,
Along with the symbolism based thereon:
And with the highest truth as nourishment for the Spirit.
Neither appearance nor image is essential – but only
That which transcends the limits of mere outward signs.

Modern science is quite far from the realm
Of this sublime spiritual light;
Apart from the things that it can measure,
Enlarge, weigh, or split, it knows nothing.

The images of the universe are infinitely diverse –
The wind of the Spirit blows where it will.

XXXII

If science does not have its crown it dries out,
Becomes sterile, and falls into nothingness –
Not without taking its revenge, which means,
Not without dragging man down with it.

Knowledge is what it should be
Only when you follow the trace of the Most High in it.
So do not fail your knowledge;
It says to you: "What am I? Give me my crown."

XXXIII

When thou standest before God, what happened previously?
Thy human activity – was it great or small?
Was it admired or not? Whatever it may have been,
It no longer exists – thou standest before the Being of God.

XXXIV

The so-called Enlightenment
Harked back to Plato and Aristotle;
For it, church and mysticism were of the past.
Nature and reason were its sole delight.
It should be ashamed of its pride –
But one cannot reproach everything in it.

XXXV

The spirit of the Enlightenment was the edge on which
I very early found the True.

I say the "edge," and not the kernel of the thing,
For never would I have forsaken my Lord.

God is not church, even if one feels it so –
One cannot confine God to dogmatics.

In some illusions, one can find a sign –
But only God can kindle love of God.

XXXVI

In time and space, a being has two limits and one content:
Birth and death, and between them life;
Body and spirit – the content is the soul.
Thou must not confuse these things.

What counts in space? Neither body nor soul,
But the Spirit, which gives everything its meaning.
What counts in time? Neither birth nor death,
But life, which offers thee the Path towards beatitude.

XXXVII

Confronted with trials in life
Say to thyself: it will be good, or better, later;
But also: the play of the world-wheel is indifferent —
Let God's providence rule on earth.

XXXVIII

Corpus, anima, spiritus:
We are *corpus*, as stones are;
We are *anima*, as animals can be;
We are *spiritus* through the wind of the Holy Ghost.

So let us do what the Spirit requires:
Where there is power, there are also duties.
The child of man belongs to the Sovereign Good.

XXXIX

Soma, psyche, pneuma: wherever the Spirit appears,
That which accompaniest it, is born of the Spirit.
The human body is spirit in its fashion
And was chosen by the Spirit to be Its symbol.
In the world, the body is the journey
Of the Spirit through earthly existence.
The body was born as a ray from the Divine Light.

XL

The worth of a man is not in his gifts,
For even the vilest scoundrel can be gifted.
The worth of a man lies in his ideas;
Whoever thinks and believes something false, esteem him not —
To the extent that he has not vanquished illusion.

On the other hand, always value in thy heart
The soul that has turned to the True.

XLI

It may be that a wicked man also has his good side —
Nevertheless, one should not ease the way for his sins.

The evil that he did and that he does,
His good sides cannot turn into good.

Certainly thou shouldst not hate a person who does evil —
But thou must always give due heed to what counts.

In principle, be well-disposed towards thy neighbor —
God grant that he be the child of good spirit.

XLII

The man in whose soul the Intellect has awoken
Can, and must, think completely independently;
Not so the pseudo-philosopher —
All he can do is to drown the truth in his foolishness.
Quod licet Jovi, numquam licet bovi:
"What is lawful for Jupiter, is not lawful for the ox."
The fool should not try to make his mark in philosophy —
One whose Intellect is deficient should not play the sage.

XLIII

One talks of "putting the cart before the horse"—
This is precisely what crude pragmatism does;
It thinks that twisting things is philosophy.
I call it simply willful satanism.
To invert everything that is natural
Is to collaborate with the devil's ruse.

XLIV

For the knights of old it was a duty
To redress wrongs on our earth —
This was the noble purpose of the hero;
The sage too must care for what is right.
The knight sought to rescue women from distress;
The sage's battle must be for the Truth.

XLV

Knights errant wanted to protect women,
But they became robbers, who used their swords shamefully.
Such a use of arms was certainly unworthy
Of their knightly initiation.
In all ages, noble heroes have become villains.
One calls this the history of the world.

The Crusades — "*Dieu le veut*" — were accompanied by atrocities
Committed even in Byzantium, though it was Christian,
Because the Crusaders knew not what God can wish —
Do not trifle with God's holy Will! What was promised
At the beginning of the Crusades never came to pass —
That which the Most High willed, had to be.

XLVI

"There is only one victor, which is God" –
This is written on the walls of the Alhambra.
For *vincit omnia Veritas*. The True
Will remain, even if nothing of the world remained.

XLVII

If He is near thee, thou shouldst nothing fear;
And likewise, thou shouldst nothing desire.
Stern words – thou must understand them aright;
Before God, let not human nature consume thee.

God knows that thou art human, and still more.
Thou art from His Spirit, though made of earth;
Be this, and also that, and yet be one –
So that thy soul, in God, may become its true self.

XLVIII

Of course one can console oneself,
But I wish to be consoled by God –
By His Truth and by His Presence,
And by the ray of His Compassion – by Him alone.

Even if our access to Him is difficult –
Ease will overcome its price.

XLIX

A man is not always in his best shape –
He may be tired, or afflicted
By the play of accident, or lack of health;
Not every jewel is well-polished.

Be forbearing and grateful; look at
What is essential – this is the measure of things.

L

One master teaches: the Most High is like light,
Like a shining inscription, on which thou gazest.
Another teaches: His Name is a sound in the heart,
From which thou canst build thy bridge.

Light is *serenitas*, sound is *certitudo*.
The two are one: *sola beatitudo*.

LI

What is Jesus? He is the Sermon of the Mount, I would say.
And what is Mohammed? The words: God is One.
And Moses? The lofty words of the Ten Commandments.
And Abraham? Prophet – before him, there was none.
He was the light and weapon of the ancient Semites.

See: all rivers flow into the ocean.

LII

The sage has two poles in his nature, but he is not split.
Shankara he must be; Krishna he may be.
Truth is everything – and Beauty is its radiation.
The sage is Truth loudly, and Beauty softly.

LIII

When thou hearest the name Krishna, thou thinkest not
Of him who sang the Bhagavad-Gita;
Nor of him whose divine form
Suddenly revealed itself in the space of things;
Thou thinkest of the one who loved the *gopis* –
And who danced with them all day and all night.

LIV

Man is *homo sapiens* and *homo faber* –
Not only one or the other;
But above all he is *sapiens*. When he saw the light of day,
He swore before God the oath of the Spirit.

As *faber*, he can make what is useful to him.
As *sapiens*, he can awaken to gnosis.

LV

Thou ask for what reason man was created,
Given that he was destined to fall.
God put His likeness into the world,
So that something divine might walk on earth.

Why then was there the forbidden tree?
For false freedom there was no room.
The world had to separate itself from God
In order to be world; thus was it written in the stars.

LVI

Poetry, music and dance – they are the language of Heaven;
Within them beauty and love, and the splendor of woman;
It is strange that what belongs to this world
Can also provoke a movement toward the Sovereign Good.
This is because what enchants us on earth,
Makes us happy because of its divinity.

LVII

Science demands pure objectivity –
It demands the elimination of everything that is "I."
But this is only one aspect of knowledge –
The other aspect is likewise a world for itself;
Seen thus, we are a web of I and thou.
True science is not only quantity –
It also requires the living "I."

LVIII

The Good has absolutely no need of its contrary,
As some maintain, in order to recognize itself as good.
For Reality is Pure Selfhood,
In which is no division.
Opposites belong to *Māyā* or appearance;
They do not penetrate into the Highest Self.

LIX

Boehme is scarcely a metaphysician;
Meister Eckhart is, although
He can exaggerate on the side of asceticism–
Yet Rome has none more profound than he.

LXI

That which is beyond good and evil
Is *ipso facto* the infinitely Good;
Who says the good, says: willingly to give oneself —
Pure Being triumphs over nothingness.

LXII

Beautiful Eve is the will to radiate, drawn from Adam's body —
Necessity took possibility as wife.

It cannot be that manifestation is mere illusion;
It is not easy to understand what existence means.

Ātmā may allow itself to be understood —
The problem of *Māyā* is more difficult to grasp.

From *Ātmā* the ray of *Māyā* emerged —
Happy are those who have found themselves in *Ātmā*.

LXIII

Doctors are not there to abolish death,
But rather to alleviate life's sufferings;
The plagues of former times were necessary
In order to eliminate all sorts of degenerations.
A late heir of Hippocrates
Was Paracelsus, who saw the root of medicine
In the web of being;

Thus all things point towards the Creator.

LXIV

Completely different is the Sacred Number
Which, for Pythagoras, meant the universe,
From the number which, for pseudo-philosophers[1],
Serves only to split hairs.

Pythagorean numbers are a symbol
Of Divinity, in order to represent the Mysteries;
Whereas the scientists' numbers only serve
To deceive those who believe in progress.

LXV

Reason, sentiment, imagination, memory,
And Intellect — from these the soul is made.
What is its content? For the soul wants to live —
Man is like a house full of people.

He likes to imagine many things,
And to think about them; not only love
Interests him, but also things in the world —
The objects of all his instincts.

But above all this is the throne of Pure Being —
That which alone is real. And thou shouldst know:
In thinking of the Word that contains all,
Thou canst lack nothing that is worth thinking about.

LXVI

Despair is the low-point of doubt:
A doubter is one who has no God.
Happiness is certitude: the primordial power
That protects the soul's ship from storms and wreck.

Certitude: God alone is Being and Salvation —
The rock of Truth, on which everything rests.

LXVII

"One should not praise the day before the evening" –
Neither should one, in the evening, criticize the day;
For if, in the evening, I am at peace,
God's providence has played its part.

LXVIII

"Give me a support in space,"
Said Archimedes, "and I can lift the earth off its hinges."
This means that he who knows the meaning of existence,
Has found the key to all the wonders of the universe.
However small the cause may be in the world –
The effect, through God, can be mighty;
And this proves: mighty was the seed –
Its smallness in the world was but appearance.

LXIX

Beauty of expression is not without meaning –
It is part of the charm of the face.
Stupid contortions of the face
Can destroy its harmony.
Equilibrium of expression is a part of dignity;
Self-domination should not be a burden.
Say not all this is but a trifle –
Barbarism is a sign of our time.

LXX

Woman was not created in order to be man;
It is because she should not be so that God created her.
And yet the sexes are not mere duality –
They are One being that bows down before God.
Man has his mission: fighting the dragon;
And woman has hers: making others happy.

LXXI

For Parmenides, there is only Being –
All else is illusion of the senses:
Lightness, heaviness; brightness, darkness.
But Reality remains untouched; it does not change.
China thinks similarly: Tao, Yin and Yang:
The Primordial Power splitting into two;
And from these two the world arises,
While the essence remains in the Ineffable.
Nevertheless, brightness is from the domain of Being;
Yin, in a sense, is like unto the Tao.

LXXII

"Feather from the Tail of the Yellow Hawk" was
My friend, the sun dance priest of the Crow;
From his eagle fan one could feel
The healing power of his good spirits.
He was a man of a childlike disposition,
And deeply penetrated by a sense of Being and of life.
Everything for him was prayer; and he faithfully sang
His song to the Great Spirit until the end.

LXXIII

What is the proof, I might be asked,
That thou art right when thou speakest of the One
Who is All – of the Great Unseen?
Might we not think that this is mere dream?
In answer, I could remain silent – or I could say:
These truths I have not received from outside;
I believe in them because I am, in the spirit, what I believe –
God help me to bear it with humility.

LXXIV

Childlikeness –
I have often thought of this happiness.
Ephemerality –
It brings a gentle sadness into this dream.

One would gladly be a child; also for God
Thou canst be such –
And happily consecrate thyself, in life and death,
To the Eternal.

LXXV

Who am I? *Brahma Satyam* – and essentially nothing else.
What constitutes my ego is mere husk;
The Path is to become That which knows Itself,
So that the heart be filled with the Self –
Just as a cup which, when empty, resounds,
And longs for its purpose – to be filled!

LXXVI

Truth; God's Presence; and with it
Compassion – this is God-Remembrance.
The answer: liberating certitude;
The fragrance of devotion; with the heart's desire
To be ready, and to give thyself to the Lord.

LXXVII

"The Lord possessed me in the beginning of His way —
I was set up from everlasting, from the beginning, or ever the earth was."
Thus speaks Wisdom in the Holy Scripture. Because before
The world was, there was the Spirit which saw all.

Wisdom, enthroned beyond becoming,
Illumined the multitude of possibilities.
The Pure Spirit — which also dwells in the sage —
Was already there, before the world existed.

LXXVIII

Man can act and man can receive;
This is symbolized by his two hands.
May God grant that, in both circumstances,
The will of man turn to the good.

The content of our activity can be good,
And what we willingly receive can be good:
It depends on *how* we accomplish our free act,
And *how* we receive.

There is not only the "what," there is also the "how."
There is not only the content, but also the manner
Of acting and receiving. Take care
That thy conduct be not praised without good reason.

LXXIX

Solomon wrote that all is vanity,
And that it is wise to scorn everything —
But not justice and piety;
For our heart should strive for nothing else .

It is vanity if we value the ephemeral
As if it were our salvation.
Justice is one with Wisdom: Thought, will, activity,
Based on Truth, are the door to eternity.

"Wisdom is the breath of God's Power,"
That knows all, and procures all good.

LXXX

A beautiful woman is a symbol of faith:
She is a "yes," and she is limitless.
And what is liberating is an intuition of greatness —
In the truly beautiful, even the small becomes great.

She is mystery, a path to the Inward;
For what she radiates is Infinity —
Only in the heart can one escape restraint.

Faith does not require letters of proof —
Its true nature is a way to inward depth.

LXXXI

Certitude and serenity — therein
Lies not wisdom alone, but also beauty;
Where there is truth, there is the fragrance of bliss —
Not only light, but also warmth is a gift.

LXXXII

Individuality is suffering — if there were no ego,
There would be nothing on earth to suffer.
It is not quite the same with happiness:
For God is Joy beyond our joys;
And he who gains beatitude, returns to his true Self.

LXXXIII

Dies irae, dies illa,
Solvet saeclum in favilla.
Thus sing the pious —
Knowing that the day must come.

But the wrathful side in God's nature
Did not exist before creation.
And the Quintessence of the song of Existence,
Is in God — it is Pure Being, Peace.

LXXXIV

To be serene is to soar above the din of the world;
From this arises another virtue:
Impassibility of soul. Thou must combine
The wisdom of old age with the intensity of youth.
Thou must not push thy heart to austerity alone;
What was childlike in thee, thou must keep.

Impassibility has nothing to do with pride;
Even in victory, thou must remain humble.

LXXXV

Vairagyānanda – "Blessèd through holy impassibility" –
This is the name of someone who wrote a book on yoga;
The book I have forgotten, but the magic of the name
Has ever remained in my memory.

Vairagya: what is past should fascinate thee no longer;
What lies in the future, is in the hands of Mahādeva.

LXXXVI

Music is wonderful, or else not so refined,
Just like people who long not for higher things.
Only from a noble source can the noble resound –
The larks sing, but the crows shriek.

Good music, from the Elysian Fields –
May it build a bridge to our heavenly home.

LXXXVII

To be a Vedantist who knows *Ātmā* and *Māyā*,
And who finds freedom and *mokṣha* in Knowledge,
Is not the same as being a Hindu
Who is bound by a thousand rules.

To be a Sufi *'ārif*, in whose heart
Allah knows Himself, is not the same as
Reading Sufi books, and then imagining
That Wisdom can be derived from the world of faith.

LXXXVIII

Is it not said: *Ex Oriente Lux*? This is true;
However — since the exception proves the rule —
It can happen, if God wills, that what is beneficial for the wise
May also come, early or late, from the West,

If God wills. Countries do not have walls —
East and West can help each other.

LXXXIX

Hindus, Christians, Moslems, and Buddhists
All pray with a rosary;
Not just once do they say the sacred Words —
But a hundred, a thousand times — they strive after totality.

The beads or knots are multiplicity;
The thread is unity — the abode of the Most High.
The many is a movement within time —
The One is the song of Eternity.

It is also said that the thread is humility —
If the thread breaks, all man's worth is lost.

XC

Blessèd be the blameless warlord,
Strong yet good, like the Sultan Saladin.
On the battlefield, he could prove his manhood –
But he readily pardoned the vanquished.

The crusaders cruelly put all to fire and blood –
They did not spare Byzantium, their brothers in Christ;
They did not want to condescend to magnanimity –
Thus their noble enemy had to put them to shame.

It is not enough to fight against injustice –
The true hero must conquer himself.

XCI

"The gods love obscure speech,"
So tells us India's wisdom. This saying explains
Why mythology and Holy Scripture
Teach the truth through bewildering images.

"Thou shouldst not give what is holy to dogs,"
Said Jesus. He who would reach the Highest Truth
Must strive towards it through Dante's dark forest.

Truth is not a tangled web of myths –
Thou carriest it, unveiled, in the depth
Of thy spirit, as it may please the Lord.

XCII

"No" to vain things, when standing before God;
"Yes" to God, to His holy nearness.
Serene dispassion, and confidence
Through the certitude that I see in my heart.

XCIII

The tree that has its root in the Truth
Shall not dry up when calumny assails it;
It may be that this tree knows not exactly what it is —
It knows what God is, in the face of every poison.

Calumny must exist in a wicked world,
But it cannot disturb Pure Being or the Spirit —
It is an honor for those whom it afflicts.

XCIV

Who art thou, man, to criticize creation?
For what is written, is what counts;
Where there are men, there must also be injustice —
Our earth should not quake because of this.

Praise be to the Creator, above all worlds.

XCV

The biggest enigma is not Necessity;
The enigma of enigmas is Possibility.
It is not the Absolute that perplexes the spirit —
It is relativity that complicates things.

What must be, is certain beyond doubt;
The breach in existence arises only in the "perhaps."
And certain is, what I say in God.

XCVI

"He who knoweth his soul, knoweth his Lord" –
He who knoweth his Lord, knoweth his soul.
Say not that a sage knows not himself –
Where God is, the star of self-knowledge shines.

XCVII

The first couple were clad in animal skins
From the moment they were cast out of Eden;
It was not their nakedness, but their souls,
That no longer were allowed to live in Paradise.

The question is: could it have been otherwise?
The right answer would be: yes and no.
Holy innocence can scarcely exist any longer
In the everyday life of society.

XCVIII

If thou standest before God, ask not: am I good?
Thy heart is good beneath the banner of the Lord.
Thou knowest that none is good but God;
Whatever I may be, the Lord is good within me.

XCIX

Thou mayst have reached a crossroad –
And knowst not whither to proceed.
It is well said that all roads lead to Rome;
But one never knows where better winds may blow.

Think on God – and go where thou wilt;
So that, with Him, thou fulfillest the right.

C

One day, a *brahmin* came to a well
Where a *pánchama*[2] sat in the sunshine;
"Give me to drink," said the brahmana;
"This I may not do," said the other,
"As thou well knowest, I am not pure for thee."

The priest: "Say: Shiva! This word
Is purification, whatever thou mayst be."

CI

Firm faith is a sure rudder;
Jesus also listened to the Roman, to the heathen:
"Thy faith hath helped thee, brother" –
Him who has faith, God leads to pastures of grace.

One pole is merit and the law –
The other is the free power of faith.

CII

Progress is the caricature of a truth, that is:
The last word belongs to the Creator alone,
To whom the first word also belonged.
Nature finds its end in the Highest Good.

CIII

Noble pride is not conceit. There is a pride
That is false, and mixed with conceit and bad will;
Thus does the worthless man seeks
To satisfy his craving for bitter pettiness.

The meaning of noble pride is: to grasp what is great –
And not allow oneself to be drawn into despicable pettiness.

CIV

It is no game to denounce what is vain –
One would prefer, in the service of truth,
To praise what is noble and beautiful.
But the stern will to rebuke error comes from Above.

CV

Christians and Saracens fought each other
To death – and did so because "God willed it."
Yes and no; God takes men as they are.
Of course He favors peace in truth –
But He is not blind to the flaws of men.

CVI

It is not easy to be highly gifted;
Life is easier without too many gifts.
But what must be done, let it be done –
The work is there, and God wishes to have His instrument.

CVII

"I am black, but beautiful"; the Truth is black
Inasmuch as it must often say "no";
"But beautiful": Truth has the fragrance of beatitude –
Thou must not carry only the *burden* of Truth.

CVIII

What is the message of the names of high nobility?
One thinks of ancestors, heroes, noble striving.
Noblesse oblige; the way of nobility
Is indeed to give the best example.
But above all its way leads inward:
To be conscious of what constitutes man;
To give one's works to the world, and oneself to the Most High.

CIX

Quite unsatisfactory — from the earliest times — was the relationship
Between princes and people; so too, on another plane,
Their relationship with religion. The time thus was ripe
For the rift — for the downfall of the world.

Men are brothers, in different social stations;
With one voice ye should call upon the Lord;
Upon the Most High, who holds you in His hand.

CX

Every human being has an existential duty —
To stand before God, and to stand before his brother;
The second is the consequence of the first;
And thy prayer is the rudder of the ship of life.

The Creator put thee on earth,
It is the Spirit that holds the world together.

CXI

It is certain that man needs the earth –
For he cannot live all alone, for himself.
And know that thy duty must be done –
For it is certain that the earth also needs thee.

The earth owes thee what thou needest;
And conversely, thou owest it thy light.

CXII

Serenitas – for everything lies in the Now,
And not in the haste which hunts thee like a wild animal.
Above the clouds, there is no time.

Then trust – because everything lies before thee;
Even before the world, God was ready for thee.
The Most High waits. He says: come to Me.

CXIII

I came into a world which did not want me –
In my earliest years, it sought to destroy me.
With God's help, I went my way –
And what had to be done, I was able to do.

Certainly, darkness has need of light;
But without God's blessing we are nothing.

CXIV

If the world of the senses is the outward,
Then the Lord, who created everything, is the inward.
Man is a microcosm, a little world.
He lives in the outward as he pleases –

In the inward alone can he reach his true being.

CXV

Seemingly good people, who do nothing to earn Heaven,
Are nonetheless evil in their own way.
It is not for nothing that one preaches:
Be ye true men – be just!

For the danger is great: certainly hell
Cannot be eternal; nevertheless it is without end
Inasmuch as man loses himself:
He becomes another being. He may obtain Beatitude
In the end – in a foreign world.

CXVI

A friend once visited a monastery of lamas,
There was a pond with fishes, colored red;
He was told: these formerly were monks –
The pond has inherited their presence.

To be a lama, then to become a fish,
Is not worth the trouble. It is astonishing
How irrational people can be,
Who are seeking liberation here on earth.

CXVII

Why are we in this earthly world?
For God; and not for this or that tiny cause.
Certainly, we must concern ourselves with small
And troublesome things; but not with trifles alone —
For the Lord is watching. Small duties come from our great Duty;
The one who loves not God, deserves not life.

CXVIII

There are two kinds of learning
Or of thinking in general: the first
Concentrates on the Essential, the One, the Center —
And this is the most rigorous and the most difficult.

The other kind consists of knowing many things —
Of casting an astonished gaze upon the possibilities
Of the universe; it is a probing, an admiring,
And also a hesitation — before unlimited spaces.

CXIX

The opposite of faith and trust
Is the pseudo-philosophy of "*Angst*" that has been
Invented: those who are no longer willing, or able, to think,
So it is affirmed, are the ones who are right.

It is obvious that "me-first" madness
Mocks intelligence and experience.
The only way to our true Self
Lies in piety — in God and Virgin Nature.

CXX

Sound logic is a guarantor of Truth;
A sharp intelligence means justice.
Morality must also be present in our thinking —
To think illogically is already wickedness.

Let not the words of the evil one trouble you,
All he does is to distort the truth.
The arch-enemy imagines you are blind to his tricks —
But for God, his talk is empty wind.

CXXI

The *pariah* type — not every outcaste —
Is a mixture of noble and vulgar traits.
It would be better for him to be a *shudra*,
Than, in appearance, to fly in the heights of the Spirit.

The pure *shudra* — not capable of greatness —
Is better than the duplicity of the *pariah*;
He is what he is, and may be very good —
He does not look enviously at the highest goal.

CXXII

God said: "Let there be light." Before this, all was dark,
Chaotic and empty. — Space is a vast night;
Light is everything. God created the universe,
And the multitude of sentient beings, for the Light.

The soul without light is without profit —
Truth and Spirit are the meaning of all things.

CXXIII

There are things that are lent and things that are given —
Those things are lent that everyone can have;
Those that are given are a sacred endowment from God
In order to counter the blindness of the world.

Despise not what is merely lent;
It may be a small building block,
Intended by God for the perfection of the world.

To respect the building-block means:
Not simply to look towards a far-off goal,
But, above all, to build thyself.

CXXIV

In his *Purgatorio*, Dante criticized women
For their low-necked robes:
He thought that the pleasure women take in the glow
Of their physical beauty was displeasing to Heaven;
He felt that St. Peter would be unforgiving.
But might not the goddess of love be indulgent?

Let one not jest regarding Heaven's measures —
God holds the scale, and He weighs the hearts.

CXXV

If thou walkest in virgin Nature, thou feelest joy
In meadows and wild forests.
Life is also thus — always going forward,
Wherever destiny may wish to guide thee.

But there is more: thou art conscious of thy path —
Thou bearest the final goal deep within thy breast;
Death, the hereafter, and the Last Judgment.

CXXVI

Is Aphrodite a reality?
Did she really arise from the sea?
She certainly arose from the sea of divinity;
She seeks, mercifully, to draw near to humanity.
She is the one whom the brahmins call Lakshmî,
And whom the sages of the West
Know as the grace and mercy of God —
The *Rahmah* of the Arabs. For everywhere
The universe lives from the radiance of the Godhead.

CXXVII

I knew a priest who was intelligent and noble,
But who died in a state of depression;
How is it possible that such a man,
At the end of his journey, was ruined and undone?
He was learned and pious, but also egoistic —
And thus his own soul betrayed him.
Happy the one who, despite worldly illusion, obtains grace.

CXXVIII

One of the greatest virtues of the soul
Is patience, based on the love of truth,
And nobility. Absurdities are
The daily bread of human agitation.

CXXIX

Man's worth lies in his love of truth.
It is love of truth that engenders nobility.
But the noble man lives in a wicked world
That all too often yields to the false,
And this he must endure day by day.
There is indeed consolation, but too much vexation;
Happy the man who is resigned to God's will.

Where there is light, there must also be shadows —
God alone gives thee absolute peace.

CXXX

There are many things thou shouldst know,
Says the evil one to me, always ready with his tricks.
I say to myself: God knows what is at stake.
What comes from the evil one, I do not wish to know.

CXXXI

Truth is the sage's heavenly bride:
The Absolute; the relative; and the Spirit.
On another plane: God, world, and soul.
Thus is the message of truth clear and complete.
What the doctrine brings us is twofold:
One is supreme, the other relative.

CXXXII

Ātmā, *Māyā*, and *jivātmā* are
The fundamental concepts that constitute wisdom:
Reality, appearance, and consciousness
With which men contemplate the true.
Consciousness, or Intellect, is made of reality
And appearance. All is *Ātmā*, Pure Being.

CXXXIII

The ternary *karma, bhakti, jñāna* —
Action, love, and knowledge — permeates
The spiritual life. Just as certitude,
Along with serenity, resounds in our spirit.

Action can be affirmative or negative;
Love is either peace or intensity, life;
Knowledge is seeing, and also being —
The striving of the spirit is many things in one.

CXXXIV

Resignation should be unconditional,
And so should trust. The presence of the Lord
Brings consolation; thou knowest that in the end
The Highest Good awaits thee in Peace.

Songs without Names

Tenth Collection

"The Lord possessed me in the beginning of His way —
I was set up from everlasting, from the beginning, or ever the earth was."
Thus speaks Wisdom in Holy Scripture;
Because, before the world was, there was the Spirit which saw all.

Songs without Names

Tenth Collection

I

Commit thy ways unto the Lord, and He will bring it to pass,
Thus it is said in Scripture. The question
Is not whether, with time, and by the play of destiny,
A good lot will befall thee;
It is that, if thou art a believer,
By God's Mercy all will be for the best.

II

Vedanta, japa, darshan — doctrine of the truth,
Invocation of the Most High,
Then contemplation of the beautiful
With a view to interiorization.
Honor be to nature, art and noble women.

III

Do not agree with the person thou lovest
Only for love's sake; be not angry
With the one thou lovest not, for no just man
Succumbs to prejudice. Stand by the truth —
Because this is the God-given duty of thy heart.

IV

The mentally sick man does not know himself,
And what he says is hardly trustworthy;
Not that he consciously falsifies things —
But his psychic life is awry.

In the psychopath, there is always a door
To the devil; but who can force him
To open it to the enemy? Where prudence reigns —
Beneath humility's heavenly banner —
The evil one's cunning will not succeed.

V

Beauty would have no sense in the eyes of God,
If it did not have a meaning for our spirit —
If it did not summon to interiorization,
To nobility, and to the abode of the Most High.

Many believe they must flee from seduction;
I am far from blaming this misunderstanding,
Because people are what they are able to be;
Fortunate are those who through beauty are ennobled.

VI

There should be no love without truth;
On truth should harmony in marriage be based.
What is alien to truth is vain and will not endure —
Only in the Spirit will you find what is lasting.
Be truthful with each other;
May God lead you to the land of Peace —
And then unite you for eternity.

VII

The difference between great and small
Means nothing for modern science;
Only energy and mass count for it.
This is the nag they ride to death.

On earth, man represents Heaven;
His vision of things manifests God's intention:
Greatness means reality and power —
It is a witness to God, Who created both great and small.

VIII

The Lord created us as his reflected image;
But reflection inverts what you see —
Thus, in a manner, man creates the Lord:
He does this through speech, and through prayer.

Unreality, ye say, because it is mere appearance;
Indeed so — but reflection must be.
And be not concerned here about heresy:
In the inward image, God is concealed.

This means: when thou pronouncest the Name of the Most High,
God Himself pronounces it. Thine own being is nothing.

IX

There are two kinds of wisdom:
Firstly the doctrine of the essence of Reality;
Then the simple wisdom for living, that consoles —
Do not despise whatever can uplift us.

X

According to Ibn 'Arabi, the mission of Noah
Was to emphasize the oneness of God;
The idols of the heathens were in reality God's Names
Which, however, had long been forgotten.
The response to Noah's doctrine is that God
Also reveals Himself in multiplicity, in the outward;
And so Noah means: the last word of Truth,
Which has its end in the All-One —
The equilibrium between oneness and radiant perfection.

The meaning of Noah's ark is the completion
Of the revelation—of the prophet's mission.

XI

Shankara and Krishna: two natures which
In the *Avatāra* are combined,
And in human perfection, manifest both aspects of God:
The Outward and the Inward.
Truth and beauty; doctrine and music;
The message of Heaven and happiness on earth.

XII

The psychic substance of the normal man
Is never split, though it may have poles;
But the misguided or sick soul
Has a chaotic and contradictory nature –
It is two "I's" on the basis of one ego.
Be one, with just complementarity;
Not two without a center – without identity.

XIII

Peace must truly be God's Peace;
On a hollow peacefulness, alien to the True,
Falls God's curse.
Blessèd is he who, with pious mind,
Combines true peace with holy war.

XIV

The size of a thing has a specific meaning –
Not just its form and color counts here below;
To every thing, every living being, is given
A particular extension in space.

It is in the nature of the proud stag
To be large, according to measures given by God;
And because the Creator's intention willed it,
The squirrel, in the eyes of us men, is small.

Here noble majesty in Heaven's wake;
And there childlikeness – nature's smile.

XV

Thinking is a good given by God;
But the average man makes no use of it.
If all men made use of it,
Then, it seems to me, there would be no world history.

XVI

"God is the Light of the heavens and the earth,"
Thus it is said in the Koran. The Lord is Light as such,
Then Light here below, wherever Truth shines;
And also in man's spirit; Light which blesses thee.

XVII

The sun is Light as a likeness;
The moon, which participates in it, is not so —
Therefore it is condemned to wane,
And to resign itself to the new moon's darkness.
Light in itself cannot disappear,
But its bearer, a mirror, can rust;
This cost Lucifer Heaven.

XVIII

St. Michael, with his sword of Light,
Stands at Heaven's gate; His opposite,
The sinister Lucifer, when he approaches,
Falls back into his self-willed night.
For *Vincit omnia Veritas* — Light alone
Can be God, and God's mighty Word.

XIX

"Thy rod and thy staff, they comfort me,"
Sings David. This does not mean
That the Most High has two staffs in His Hands;
It means that, in dark times,
His shepherd's crook is our best help. —
The repetition of the image is Semitic,
A mere reinforcement, intended to lead us to the true meaning.

XX

In walking, one puts one foot before the other;
So too in life's wayfaring, day by day —
A rotation. For to go forward in the Spirit,
Means standing before Thee, beyond all time.

XXI

With peoples, until the most recent times,
There was a tendency toward totality, toward the Absolute –
In spirituality, on the earthly plane,
And also in penal law, in the misuse of the rod.

Not without greatness is the tendency toward the harsh –
But it is petty when, on that account, men bleed to death.

XXII

The world of men? It has fallen quite low –
Tell me how it was a thousand years ago.
That it had faith, much nobility,
Monasticism, and chivalry – is clear.

The East is the magical world of the sacred –
What it can offer us is wonderful.
But that it too is human, all-too-human,
Far from the sacred and even hostile to it, is crystal clear.

XXIII

We know from experience that in our lives
Something suddenly becomes quite different.
We no longer know – or so it seems – who we are.
Let us be what we must be, in the Name of the Most High.

If many things in life change,
Take courage. God is the Good Shepherd.

XXIV

Corruptio optimi est pessima –
One thinks too readily of the fall of the angels,
But true celestial beings cannot fall –
He who falls was already in the evil one's grip.
The fall of the angels was invented
In order to provide an image of pride.

XXV

The worst corruption is the corruption of the best,
Says a proverb. The truly good
Cannot perish, for what can be corrupted
Carries within itself the possibility of dying.
Fallen spirits wanted to be divine –
They were true angels only in appearance.

XXVI

Some people think in terms of black and white;
For instance: if a potentate dies,
The eldest son decapitates the younger ones,
Lest a foolhardy brother – who can tell? –
Might be tempted by the pleasures of governance and fame;
Such atrocities are the sad price
Of world history and ethnology.

The opposition between black and white does have a meaning –
But not if one breaks the demands of Truth.

XXVII

Someone wants to be God, because he accords himself false rights;
Consider the case of Icarus, who fell into the sea.
Another seeks to become one with the Highest Self,
Because God's Selfhood has ordained this as his destiny.

Quod licet Jovi — says an old saying —
Non licet bovi. Stay in thy place,
Where the grace that is appropriate for thee shines.

XXVIII

Man is activity, and his best action
Is the one that has the Divine as its content.
For whatever expresses the Highest Self
Is the very Word thereof — is God's own Act.

Without God thou canst not think what is divine —
But God thinks within thee, and will give thee Light.

XXIX

Avalokitéshvara is without sex;
But for Far-Easterners, he becomes Kwan-Yin,
The goddess of mercy. His nature
Sows Heaven's luminous seeds in masculine or feminine form,
According to the ray of God's splendor.

XXX

People who like agitation readily say that
Man exists as long as he does something.
To this I answer: yes and no. Man is man
To the degree that he reposes in the Divinity;

And therein lies indeed a certain activity —
Without activity, thou canst not move toward God.

XXXI

When the shadow of a pariah falls upon them
Many Hindus believe it to be a deadly poison.
But impurity comes not merely out of the air —
Exaggeration can also poison the soul.

XXXII

Purifying oneself — from what? From false action;
But also from the manner in which we act, whether wrongly or justly.
And likewise from receiving: for not only the content counts;
The way and manner in which we receive also may be good or bad.

Thy path is woven of "what" and "how" —
Seek what is pure in the heart's alchemy.
Giving and taking is human life —
In both, thou shouldst uplift thy soul.

XXXIII

Thy Name tells me that Thou art unique.
My thinking brain is universal space, *Māyā*;
The dream becomes silence when Thy Word resounds;
And whatever good I think, testifies to *Ātmā*.

XXXIV

The sun's orbit is but appearance; for the sun stands still,
It is Center. But it has been discovered
That the sun too is not motionless in space –
That it has a movement, towards the limitless.

Appearance or reality? The opposition here is relative.
Because we do not call real
What is a fixed thing; only
What we know perhaps a little better.

In the Pure Spirit alone dwells complete knowledge –
That which, coming from God, we must know.

XXXV

Primordial certitude is the value of values;
On it, essentially, all knowledge depends.
And even if we cannot know everything –
Trust in God stands on solid ground.

Reason and faith should meet –
And may the Most High make smooth our ways.

XXXVI

Thou wishest to be where thou canst experience
This or that beneath the banner of the world;
Better to be within one's heart, wherein is the meaning of life –
For what is worthy of living is here, is here.

This is what counts when thou standest before thy Creator –
Nevertheless God made the world for thee.
Prayer and world are not always opposites –
Because God also put Himself into the world.

XXXVII

All too often philosophy is the thinking
Of a "no-longer-wishing-to-think," and not a reflection
On what is the essential content of all thinking;
One entertains thoughts that dissolve into nothingness.

True thinking leads to a reality;
But people want to replace this with the cult of existence —
A cult of power, of life. Or again:
One imagines one has unraveled the Veil of Isis.

XXXVIII

Music is melody and rhythm,
And also mood. Technical perfection
Is hardly music, for over-orchestration
Gives the message a falsified garment.

XXXIX

What one paints should preferably be static —
Because the surface on which one paints has no life.
And what one paints must be noble and refreshing —
For the purpose of painting is to offer a value.

A sacred painting is like a ray from Heaven —
It should console and uplift the soul.

XL

The laws of art are determined
By the medium and the content. The main thing
Is what is expressed or portrayed — it should be uplifting,
Useful and rejoicing, and remove our cares.
Music and the visual arts: for hearing and seeing;
Poetry: for mental understanding.

XLI

Poems — let them sing, but let them also teach;
They should increase not only our joy of living, but also our knowledge.

Further: thou canst give something good in every sphere —
But thou canst not always soar in the highest one.

XLII

The Trinity: trinity is God,
But God is not three, for in Himself He is One,
And yet He is All — He, the Highest Good.
His Name be praised eternally.

XLIII

Why are there so many religions?
Because God talks to men, not to angels.
If there were only one religion in the world,
Humanity, precisely, would not be human.

One could ask a hundred, a thousand questions;
The way to truth is both short and long.
Why does troublesome man exist?
Always this answer: All-Possibility.

XLIV

Not everything in Heaven is as it is on earth —
Certainly, in Heaven, one cannot be deceived;
Never has the Lord broken His given word —
He always gives more than He has promised.

God does not abandon those who love Him —
Does not a voice within our heart say: Here am I.

XLV

The earth revolves – hence day and night;
And it is tilted – hence the four seasons.
See how the Lord has created the order
That helps us traverse existence,
Without our seeing what His reasons are.

We stand in the mechanism of the world like a child;
In its limits and its limitless expanses –
In space, wherein life flows toward God.

XLVI

On the one hand, I say: consider the play of the world –
How wondrously it is ordained;
On the other hand, I say: leave the world alone –
You have but one duty: the vision of God.

Think, at its proper time, of each of these ways;
With an undivided heart be ready for God.

XLVII

God manifests Himself in man,
And man manifests the Lord through prayer;
Everything in this world is activity – even when
Man stands inwardly before the Most High –

Contemplating without acting. For in activity,
Our soul must repose in the First Mover.

XLVIII

Lightness, fire, and dark heaviness —
Sattva, rajas, and *tamas*, the three fundamental tendencies
From which *Māyā*'s fabric is woven;
The world arises from their combination.

The third tendency is not merely evil;
It can also be the necessity of destruction.
For if the Creator never said "no,"
He could not liberate the soul of man.

XLIX

For Christian sensibility, the body means sin;
For the Moslem, it is good and bad;
But for the Hindu it is, rather, divine —
The sage does justice to the essential content.

Clothing is a Name of God, or a dignity;
But it may also be used to cover sin.
The human body is the image of God —
Sacred nudity allows Divinity to shine.

L

Red Indians loved the profound words of Jesus —
People sowed amongst them the seed of the Good News;
But what they brought at the same time
Was an accursed framework of existence,
A vile deceit called "civilization,"
Which, instead of manifesting God's way, mocked all truth.

The opposition between culture and savagery
Has sometimes a meaning, but mostly it does not;
Too often, someone who should remain silent,
Judges those who are far better than he.

LI

When, O man, thou thinkest of God, understandest thou not
That thy prayer is more than thy countenance —
More than thine individual ego, more than the whole world?
For in prayer God is active in thy heart.

LII

Eating, drinking, sleeping, loving,
Working, praying, pleasures too;
Part-animal and part-divine —
We are men with both these natures,
Because God fashioned
Us for a double life —
And man, whatever be his individual nature,
Has but one meaning: to rise Upward.

LIII

Think not that animal nature is always base:
Eating — ambrosia is the food of Heaven;
And drinking — nectar is the beverage of the gods;
Also, one speaks of the sleep of the just;
And, as the sage knows, love bespeaks the Most High.

O friend of God, remember these things
When thou must resign thyself to what is animal.

LIV

Do not consider distant
What God has placed in your hand and heart.
The miseries of your soul should remind you
Of what, in life's struggle, you may forget:
The invisible, God-given Here.
As an old proverb says: If there is a paradise on earth,
Then it is near, it is with thee.

LV

In case ye should wish to know:
De gustibus non est disputandum.
For no reasonable person puts personal taste,
And what is good and true in itself, in the same bag.
The question is not what we find good –
Only what is good in itself should kindle our love.
One may err in one's own instincts –
But not in what God's angels love.

LVI

Mother earth should be sacred to us –
She is made for us, and we are made for her.
Likewise: the body should be sacred to us –
Its magic, woven of symbols.

LVII

Thanks to the grace of thy destiny,
A spark fell miraculously into the stream of thy soul.
It shines, unaffected by thy *Māyā* –
It is nothing other than *Ātmā. Om.*

LVIII

Thy Name is a wondrous sound
And yet stillness;
So let my heart open itself, that it may
Be filled with light.
My word, O Lord, is prayer — a deep sound
And yet silence;
And may my heart through Thy Grace
Turn toward the inward.

LIX

The noble man wishes to fulfill his duty —
He lives in God, he is "twice born."
Not so the fool — whoever wants pleasure
Only for pleasure's sake, has lost himself.

For if thou wishest to live, then breathe God's Will.

LX

It is wicked to steal a divine right —
See how Prometheus had to suffer for this.
Right is to become what the Self requires —
What It forever knew within thy heart.

LXI

Thou needst not ponder over this, O man, —
For what must be, will be.
May the Lord pour for thee the wine of Truth —
Then canst thou relinquish the burden of vain brooding.

LXII

Even if I am weak, I cannot be lost,
For God within me cannot perish.
So despite everything, I remain upright –
Even though the world should disappear, I know not when.

LXIII

If we say "transience," we always think of
The passing of things we love;
Likewise in space: "separation" is that
Whose departure saddens our soul.
On the other hand, the passing of sorrow is welcome;
And in space, that we no longer see the bad.

LXIV

It is said that everything on earth
Is imperfect. Yes, but also no –
For without manifestation of the Divine
This world could not be real.

Thou canst certainly see the good and the beautiful
In the world. So look upon it with a noble gaze –
See God's intention, see what is essential;
And find thy happiness in gratitude and in God.

LXV

Beauty is worldly and vain, some think –
See how Truth is crudely distorted
When one does not see that in every beauty
Lies also the consolation of greatness.

LXVI

That man becomes small who lives only from the small –
From what is mass, fashioned with cunning;
Iron and fire, hellish magic –
Woe unto him who confuses good and evil.

Truth, greatness, and beauty: these remind us
Of mankind's essence, deep within –
They are the soul's God-willed melody.

LXVII

The Creator gave us freedom,
So that He could lift us above our animality,
Not so that we could be brutish, and misuse freedom,
And thereby live far below the animals.

To be free: not like animals, in blind desire,
But in performing our duty as human beings –
Namely, in striving towards our essential nature.

LXVIII

Duty is what gives meaning to our earthly life –
That to which the Lord has directed our heart's path;
Duty is not what contradicts this meaning –
And destroys in us man's right to existence.

For what purpose are we born on earth?
So that our soul may become the heir to Heaven.

LXIX

The colored decoration of the body — tattooing
With a sacred intention — is more than ornamentation.
Half garment, half nakedness, the painting of the body
Manifests the person's being and radiation.

Vishnu and Shiva: each has his sign
With which the pious adorn their bodies.
The yogi, always ready to love the Self,
Inscribes his God on his body.

LXX

Red Indians have their war, hunting, and friendship dances,
And then the Sun Dance, to heal the earth.
See how the people, dancing back and forth,
Are actually running to their inward depth.

In the Sun Dance, the tree is the center,
And magically draws unto itself the dancers' steps.
Every dance is a striving towards depth —
As if the Great Spirit were calling us to Him.

LXXI

The river of life flows on day by day.
God loves and blesses those who are patient —
Those who pay homage to God's compassion
With resignation and hope in their heart.

With patience comes hope — both flow
From a light wherein an angel greets us.

LXXII

Man is body and soul. Not only this –
He is also a destiny. Not only old age and death,
But also a particular karma. For what a man is
In his core, he must inherit in his outward life.
Man is not only what thou see'st before thee –
He is also a destiny that no eye can see.

LXXIII

The White man is creative beyond limit –
He ended up flying to the moon.
The Yellow man is creative in himself –
He wishes to embellish, but not to distort.
The Black man, as you know, is a dancer –
He lets the earth be as it is.

Eastern Whites[1] constitute a world
That contains something of both east and west.

LXXIV

Truth, someone said, is not consolation,
It is mere information, it need only be true;
If nevertheless some find in it consolation,
This is only because they put their feelings into it.

This is more false than true. God is Compassion;
He does not let His poor depart empty-handed.

LXXV

In some fashion, we are always in a dark valley —
The soul's journey through the night is difficult.
God has commanded patience and trust —
He is the Good Shepherd. What more dost thou want?

LXXVI

"There is no power or strength except in God"—
Thus spake the Prophet. Why this repetition?
One is not speaking of two different things;
The two words merely emphasize the meaning.
Just as in the Psalm: "Thy rod and thy staff":
God sent us only one great consolation.

Nevertheless, two meanings are contained therein —
The Semitic spirit likes to express itself thus.

LXXVII

It is a fact that even great men do not always
Seem to be much in the eyes of other people.
Cicero wrote: I once had a visitor,
Who was as boring as an all-too-long book.
Who was the man that he was obliged to receive?
It was Caesar, who wished to speak with him.

LXXVIII

The judge Joshua is supposed to have halted the sun;
Mohammed is supposed to have split the full moon;
In Fatima, the sun apparently moved.
Miracles for the eye, for Grace placed itself there —
Not miracles of the cosmic powers.

If God were to push the sun aside,
Not much would remain of the earth.

LXXIX

Discernment between Reality and appearance;
The spirit's concentration on the True;
Together with nobility of soul for God —
The spiritual path cannot be otherwise.

Nobility: humility and trust in God —
You cannot contemplate the True in any better way.

LXXX

Like man and woman are thought and music —
Reason and song. Between the two is poetry:
Poetry is melodious thought —
Rays from the harmony of the spheres.

Sometimes the spirit is satisfied with words alone —
But sometimes, when the element love is present,
Words wish to be united with song.

LXXXI

The foolishness of some people can upset us –
It is regrettable if it makes us angry,
And continues to trouble us, for our heart is weak;
But it cannot be otherwise on earth.

LXXXII

The cosmic play is simultaneously good and bad:
It is good because it is God's manifestation;
God grant that what bears witness to Him
May deliver us from what separates from Him.

The play of the world is not God: in this sense
It is a nothingness that bows down before the All.

LXXXIII

Go trustfully towards thy God –
Māyā turns the world-wheel anyway.
God knows whither thou goest – God brings the soul
That loves Him to this very love.

LXXXIV

If you speak of *Māyā*, be careful –
For Jesus said: only God is good.

On the other hand, you cannot prevent the Lord from
Manifesting Himself to His children in the world.

What unmistakably manifests Him
Is He Himself – His Word; whether loud or soft.

LXXXV

I am not much a friend of myths –
They contain far too much that is arbitrary;
One wonders for what possible reason
Details blot out the deep meaning.

The gods, it is said, love obscure speech, so much so
That the meaning of the myth is almost extinguished.
Not everything in the life of Krishna is clear –

But behold the *gopis*, who dance round the god
To the magical sound of his drunken flute,
In the dance of love, until the red dawn.

Myth is an edifice with many levels –
Otherwise the soul could not call upon Krishna and Ram.

LXXXVI

Sometimes thou wishest that time would pass more quickly,
And sometimes, rather, that it would stand still.
But when God is near thee, thou art forever now –
So wish not that destiny decree otherwise.

LXXXVII

If the play of the cosmic dream poisons thy soul,
Take refuge in the Eternal Center:
In thy heart is the kernel of Truth –
The point where Isis lifts her veil.

LXXXVIII

The Supreme Name is a sacrament,
In whichever language it may resound.
God conceals Himself in the form of the Word,
And carries our heart through the night
On uncreated wings, until the Eternal Morning.

LXXXIX

Purification, enlightenment, and protection —
These are granted thee by the God-given Symbol.
It should be inscribed on thy forehead and in thy heart;
On thy wall and on the door of thy house.
Purity says no, and enlightenment says yes;
And, with the Lord, there is always protection.

XC

What comes from God, leads to God;
Likewise, what leads to Him,
Comes from Him.
A path from the Lord to the Lord —
This is the journey inscribed in our heart —
Blessèd are those who love the Most High!

XCI

It is said that humility is the greatest virtue.
What is humility? Resignation to
God's wish, and also trust.
Whoever knows this not, does not have faith.

Be ready for the highest Will with joy —
With eagerness. Because the heart's yes to God
Is thy life. Now and in eternity.

XCII

"The Lord is with thee" – a mighty word;
Thus the Holy Virgin was never alone.
Blessèd is the heart that is the bearer of God –
A more beautiful greeting from Heaven cannot be.

XCIII

People tell me of an immense comet
That is returning after five thousand years;
I no longer want to hear of such numbers,
Such dimensions in cold, black space.

The earth was given to me as a mother;
I would not live in the realm of the comets.
The greatest thing created is within myself –
"If there is a Paradise on earth, it is here."

XCIV

Of the enigmas of space, my mind wants not to hear;
Let them fascinate those who are tired of the earth.
Be thou with the wise who are grateful to God
For being children of good mother earth.

In this home that He has given thee –
And not elsewhere – God has quenched thy heart.

XCV

Astronomy – I do not wish to blame it;
All worlds bear witness to the Highest Creator.
The question is how we look at the All –
And whether or not we despise our world,
Because it seems too little for us. Do not forget:
The truly great thou canst not measure.

XCVI

There are thoughts that make us happy,
In the realms of both duty and love.
But nothing makes us happy like silence in God –
The holy stilling of all our desires.

Certitude, and with it Peace, are contained
In this silence – let the Divinity reign.

XCVII

It was in my early childhood –
The golden Buddha in the Japanese gallery
Was for me the image of the Great Transcendent,
The Holy One, that filled me with devotion.
Likewise, the great song of the *Gītā*
Was a grace that stilled my youthful longing.

XCVIII

In every love there is a spark of fear –
In the noble soul, love entails respect;
It is not pleasing to God that man,
Through his greed, misses the meaning of love.

Thou canst not love the Highest Good
If, in thy heart, there is no holy fear.
And I forget not the gaze of Shaikh Ahmad –
In it were fear of God and bliss in God.

XCIX

The soul first is untamed and wild –
But the Spirit's strength destroys the soul's wrath.
It becomes submissive, wishes to give of its best
And sees the world in a new light.

Some are born with this light –
The Spirit chose them from the beginning.
Blessèd the heart which, ere the world was,
Swore fidelity and love to the Most High.

C

The didactic poems have now become innumerable –
It all began, it seems to me, hardly two years ago.
I did not desire it; I often wished to stop –
Obedience is not responsible for the marvelous.

I thought I had already said everything –
But day by day new light came from above.
What could I do? For me one thing alone remains:
To praise God with patience and gratitude.

CI

The guarantee of a good future is thy "now" in God;
So go life's way with trust.
If the Lord be with thee,
The wheel of cosmic play may turn as it will.

CII

The world-wheel may turn as it will —
It does not need me, this I readily know.
And I do not need it — for my soul is at rest
In its meeting with the Lord.

On the other hand — and I say it without jest:
The world-wheel also turns within my heart.

CIII

Powerful in man is consciousness —
It is a mirror created by the Most High;
It can carry within itself things and creatures —
And God; this is the vocation of the human soul.

When metal receives the ray of the sun,
Then it is sun — luminous and immutable.

CIV

I-consciousness has various meanings:
It is to know who and where I am.
It is also to know that my heart,
In its essence, strives towards Heaven.

CV

There is a solace from God beyond all argument –
For God proves Himself without explanation;
If thou wouldst but listen to the Being of the Most High,
Thou canst protect thyself from all sorrow.

CVI

Something I have often wished to say: it is not essential
That we understand consolation in detail;
It is essential that – with the grace of faith –
We let ourselves be consoled by the Name of the Most High.

CVII

Consolation as such is God. Also consoling is, on another plane,
The conscientious performance of our duty;
Then everything that is right and good in the world –
And then the celestial unveiling of beauty.

The splendor of heaven and earth is contained in God –
As well as in the deepest folds of the human heart.

CVIII

Neither completely animal nor completely divine – just human;
Thus do we live in this world,
And wonder what, essentially, we are.

To be man is to flee from oneself to God.

CIX

A thunderstorm bears witness to God's wrath;
Hail is like His punishment. Mild rain
Shows His mercy; and pure snow
Is heavenly light — and may its blessing,
Like a white veil, cover our homeland;

The stillness of pure Being, as far as I can see.

CX

The path to the Highest Good is a bridge;
I wander clad in my earthly form
Over the river of this world, but I hear it not —

For the ground of my heart carries God's silence.

CXI

Three times does Dante portray woman:
Firstly the divine Mary;
Then the holy Beatrice; and then Matilda,
Who won Dante's attention by her nobility.

Three women did the poet describe —
Three ways to love the eternal feminine.

CXII

The Holy Virgin is primordial and universal woman;
Thus she is also cosmic compassion.
She holds the homeless one like her child
In her divine and motherly arms.

CXIII

Happiness is synonymous with certitude –
It is knowledge of God and of eternal life.
Ye say: are there not other kinds of happiness? Bethink:
Without this one, there can be none.

CXIV

The greatness of the Divinity and the faith of man:
Our trust says "yes" to the Highest Might.
But sometimes it happens, and it is very strange,
That our faith creates our Divinity –
It does so because the Lord is immanent in things,
And rewards us for the strength of our faith;

For, over all things, God's grace keeps watch.

CXV

I was once in a monastery and, on the wall,
Was painted: *memento mori*.
And rightly so: for wise thinking about dying
Unites us with our essence –
And with the life that we inherit in God.

CXVII

In the Name there is more power than in God Himself –
This is what one hears from certain zealots,
But not from the wise: to be a hero,
There is no need to delude oneself with nonsense,
Even if an ideal seduces one's mind.
Give God the honor that belongs to Him alone.

CXVIII

The world would be all right for me –
With its meadows and forests, their adornment of flowers,
And above them, the limitless sky –
If only nothing happened in the world!

CXIX

The Persian Zarathustra sees the world
As being divided into good and bad,
Light and darkness. At the end of the struggle,
A messiah comes to deliver all.

The message of Jesus, in its form,
Derives from the same quintessential idea of faith:
Here too, after a long struggle between the two powers,
A Savior came and vanquished.

Plato and Shankara – they are the same
Archetype in the realm of *Sophia*.

CXX

There are the elect, who must kindle
The light of the Spirit – even though one wants it not;
Messengers relentlessly assailed by the evil one –
God gives them victory over illusion.

"Truth has come – vain works have vanished."

CXXI

Pythagoras and Abraham: primordial Fathers –
One kindled the light of wisdom;
The other taught the law and prayer,
And brought faith to the human heart.

If you look in the mirror of history
You see Greeks here, and Semites there –
Each brought their own form of the Spirit;
Both of them built our world.

CXXII

Circle, spiral, and star –
Each one means God, world, and soul.
See how, in simple signs, I tell you
Of the nature of all that is real.
The circle shows the perfect in itself,
Without beginning, without end, without outward or inward;
Through the star and the spiral, we gain
Insight into the structure of the universe.

Geometry is the adornment of dialectics –
In it one sees without analytical thinking.

CXXIII

Man proposes, God disposes – a saying which,
Day by day, I like to keep in mind.
Mine are desires and so are fears –
Compassion and giving are God's.

CXXIV

Prophets also have trials,
For they too pass through this earthly life,
In the realm of outward things – yet their passage
Is a timeless standing before the Lord.

CXXV

Thou art my Creator, and I call on Thee –
I know Thou art my shepherd and my help;
If Thy Name resounds, all is well –
For all existence rests within Thine essence

Which is eternally One in its Selfhood.

CXXVI

Be not surprised that Heaven remains silent,
Since the power of understanding is at thy disposal;
For reason is the miracle God gave thee from the start,
And it makes thee a human being.

CXXVII

Certainly, man has the right to a sentient ego –
But this ego should not be in the foreground;
Whatever thou may'st feel or desire, thy deeper self
Must abide in the shining heights of Truth –
Blessèd the man who has escaped from his delusion.

CXXVIII

Brahma satyam — everything else is *Māyā;*
It should be indifferent to thee what the fates weave.

Brahma satyam: since this is a certainty,
Your eternal life is also a certainty.

CXXIX

Serenity and certitude are the two poles
Of our spiritual happiness and well-being.
Serenity is soaring in the heights;
Certitude is deep rootedness where I stand.
Such is the tree of the Spirit: high flight in the free air —
And, in the depth of the heart, the being of Truth.

CXXX

Candles are burning in a sanctuary:
Take to heart their motionless shining —
Remembering the Most High, the Only Real,
And confering on thy surroundings the nearness of God.

CXXXI

If thou wilt not journey to the summit for thyself,
Then be compassionate — do so for others.
What holds earth and Heaven together
Is prayer — thou owest this to the world.

Songs without Names

Eleventh Collection

There are two kinds of wisdom:
Firstly the doctrine of the essence of Reality;
Then the simple wisdom for living, that consoles —
Do not despise whatever can uplift us.

Songs without Names

Eleventh Collection

I

A proverb says: every beginning is difficult.
This is true – but a beginning can
Also be easy: if the Holy Ghost,
With God's grace, flows into thy pen.

II

Anything that opposes God is mere appearance:
A nothingness that has some existence must be;
This is willed by the infinity of Possibility.
In the realm of universal illusion there is perfection
Only in Totality. For the Good in itself is without flaw –
So it is now, and so it ever shall be.

III

What is ephemeral has already passed,
And what is everlasting thou canst see now;
The good is the manifestation of the Most High –
And what manifests nothingness should be indifferent to thee.

Remain in God and let the earth turn.

IV

After a particularly beautiful day, there came,
Without any reason, a difficult and completely different night.
Yet it was clear why:
The evil one had also thought of thee.

The enemy's guile should not disturb thee –
For what he gains here, he loses in the hereafter.

V

Morning shivers over the cypresses —
Night, with its dreams, is gone.
I did not forget God in my dream —
I forgot only who I am.

It can happen thus many a night:
Thou hast dreamt of wisdom and prayer —
And God must have heard. All else
Has been swept away by the morning wind.

Real is not what thy soul invents —
Real is what unites thee with God.

VI

The beauty of flowers is a cosmic miracle —
Heaven has strewn itself upon the earth;
With this splendor of colors in the green meadows,
God has renewed the earth's gray raiment.
High above shines the golden light of the sun —
Sometimes even earth is allowed to be Heaven.

And the wonders that you see on earth
Are a grace that penetrates the soul.

VII

The dance of the dervishes is truth and music:
Truth, because it bears witness to the Highest Being;
Music, because it brings the believing soul
Back to its essence, to Paradise.

It is not enough merely to think the True —
Ye must also give yourselves to the Divine Truth.

VIII

Intolerant or tolerant?
I am intolerant if it is a question of truth;
But I am tolerant, because the brilliance of the Divine Truth,
Shines, like the sun, in every direction.

IX

The sun lovingly gives us light and warmth;
And God, from His Pure Being, gives us truth and love.
Thou wast created in God's image;
So thou too must give from what God has given thee —
And what thou givest, thou above all must be.

X

From the Emperor Fo Hi came the trigrams —
Eight signs that contain the whole world;
They have their roots in the Highest Divinity —
And also in the deepest folds of our hearts.
I cite them as an example of those Scriptures
That lift the dark veil from the Mysteries;
And may God reign in our spirit.

XI

You look at your hands and feet —
But your face you cannot see.
You know surely you art not another —
Yet the enigma of the ego you cannot understand.

XII

The world's fabric is so strange:
Everyone thinks that he alone is "I";
Yet he sees and believes that there are others,
And that the whole dream flows into the past.

XIII

Remain at the center.
Right and left concern thee not;
This is spiritual contentment — and serenity of thy soul.

Live toward the inward;
For the outward world no longer is;
This is trust in God — certitude is beatitude.

XIV

God; the Prophet; the soul. God is the meaning of everything.
He is the Truth, Presence, and Helper,
To whom the soul's prayers are due.
Then the Prophet round whom the world is gathering,
And whom thou veneratest. And then the soul,
Which is freed by the alchemy of faith.

XV

Souls that walk on a false path
Would like to enter into another ego —
When it is too late — and be free from all sin;
What one has made of oneself, one must be.

Thou art not master over the end of times —
While it is still early, make good wine.
Have not many, as if overnight,
Made of their souls a home for God?

XVI

"Joy, beautiful spark of the gods,
Daughter of Elysium" —
Thus did a poet sing —
But without knowing why;
For joy within time
Cannot lead to any goal.
What is joy? Thou canst know it
Only in the wake of the Most High.

XVII

Love of one's neighbor is not and expansion
In society, in the everyday world;
It is a natural generosity —
What holds the human world together.

In nobility there is discretion;
For we can give only if we live in the One.

XVIII

Beauty has many modes of manifestation:
There is the God-created human body —
Woman bears witness to the essence of beauty.

And there are other ways that point to Heaven:
Poetry — which is both thought and music;
And then, in the same psychological realm,
The magic of music — be it song,
Flute, or the sweet sound of strings.

Then Nature, wherein reigns God Most High;
And art, whereby Adam created a world,
As God wills, for man has nothing from himself —

To the Primordial Source be eternal praise.

XIX

Only he who is inwardly poor for the Lord
Can be rich for others, and be their star.
Do not squander thyself because of a misunderstood teaching
About love of one's neighbor; God gives light and grace
So that thy heart may belong to Him and not to the world.

XX

Nobility of speech is of the highest value,
Because in it one honors God and one's ancestors.
On account of language the Bedouins punished
Children — and their parents thanked them for it.
If a child wished to achieve position and honor,
He was obliged, in order to learn more noble language,
To live for a time with the sons of the desert.

If thou wouldst inherit the ancestors' spirit and virtue
And transmit them faithfully to the next generation,
Then take care not to corrupt the language.

XXI

Languages have the right to change
If new spiritual values require it;
With Cicero's political Latin,
Dante could not have achieved his end.

XXII

Virgil had a childlike nature,
And was at the same time a profound visionary;
In the sage, the gift of the Spirit is combined,
Deo juvante, with goodness of heart.

XXIII

Darshan is yoga through seeing and hearing –
It is contemplation with the senses;
Blessèd art thou if thou canst obtain
Deepest knowledge even through the outward.

XXIV

Why, in the songs of Red Indians and Cossacks,
Is there a primordial power
That combines melancholy and joy of living?
What is it that creates this savage beauty?

The heroic soul combines opposites:
A storm that sweeps over prairies and waves;
Then contemplativity, a noble longing –
An inward vision, profound and motionless.

XXV

Shri Shankara, in a sense, is Vedanta –
But Vedanta is not Shrī Shankara.
Vedanta is the Truth and the Self,
And nothing else. *Om namah shivāya.*

XXVI

Shankarāchārya was hostile to the world of *Māyā*,
Yet he said: the liberated one
Is joyous with the joyful, and sad with
The sorrowful who have no consolation;
He also said: if the one liberated from illusion
Plays with children or with women,
His heart — whatever be the appearance —
Is, in its deepest core, on the side of Truth.

Whoever understands *Māyā* is eternally free.

XXVII

Wine is what makes our soul drunk:
The profound happiness of
Resignation in God, and trust in God.
Lofty serenity, and the deep power of certitude in the heart.

XXVIII

God of all men, be my Good Shepherd,
So that my feet may not wander in darkness;
God of all souls, help the one who is weak,
So that his striving toward Thee be blessed.

Whatever one thinks, whatever one does —
If only one's heart reposes in God's Being.
So give the Lord thy thinking and non-thinking —
God will direct thy soul on true paths.

XXIX

The idolatrous priests on the holy mountain –
Were but dwarfs beside Elias.
The smoke of the sacrifice made by the prophet
Rose up to Heaven – God gave victory to His friend.
So make a sacrifice in thy heart for Truth –
From the Lord thou wilt receive victory and salvation.

XXX

If thou art with God, thou art everywhere and always:
Thou art outside space and time –
Thereby also in every "here" and "now,"
In the limitless-limited dream of *Māyā*.

XXXI

All-Possibility: the Divine willed to mirror Itself
In the animal – and so we came to be.
God created man in His own image –
We are half heavenly spark and half animal.
God shows Himself in man's countenance;
Neither animal – nor earth – profanes this miracle.

XXXII

"God is Real, the world is appearance;
The soul is not other than Highest Being."
Thy first guiding maxim. This one comes next:
"Beauty is the splendor of the True."

Shankara and Plato; what they said
Was forever inscribed in thy heart.

XXXIII

What I am, I must be. I would gladly
Have been fashioned as simply as others,
But God gave me the heavy burden of my nature
Along with my duty, and said to me: now, go thy way.
And He wrote these words on the door of my heart:
Be without fear – the Most High is with thee.

XXXIV

Psychic fog that encumbers the soul –
Ignore it, and remain in the clarity
Of the Spirit. Inconstant and deceitful
Is the fog of the world. Truth is crystalline.

XXXV

It is curious how the body needs sleep,
And also the soul; then from the east comes the day.
And after thy day, with its existential din,
Thou too hast a right to a draught of non-existence.

XXXVI

Ye should not be foolishly concerned
With the body, says the ascetic.
But who is it who walks upon the earth,
And whom ye know not? He carries the remembrance of God.

XXXVII

In Heaven, the soul has the vision of God –
But it is not forbidden other vision:
The angels, saints, and all who were close to us,
Are transfigured in the one vision of God.

XXXVIII

The beauty of a man forsaken by God
Remains alien to his soul. Beauty in itself
Belongs to the Lord, and bears witness to Him;
It is no wonder that Plato compared beauty to truth.

XXXIX

The average man is but a fragment; complete men
Are rare. For the human being must have everything
That God has willed: selflessness in thinking and willing;
And the best of all gifts –

The urge to give one's inmost heart to the Lord.

XL

The visionary's message, the lofty words of the Veda:
Brahma is real, the world is appearance.
Krishna-nature, out of *Māyā*'s possibilities:
To be a human ray of divine Nature.

XLI

All-Possibility – the world is a web
Of possibilities that colorfully intertwine;
Thou wishest to call each thing by its name –
But all that thou knowest is in suspense.

Categories there are, and none is new to thee;
But the Creator of things remains free in everything.

XLII

There is a mountain: a snow-covered peak,
And down below the hermit's cell;
In heaven's nearness, serenity shines –
Within the heart, the divine essence has its home.
Height and depth are two possibilities
Of the vision of God – and two beatitudes.

XLIII

Thou art in God; God is in thee.
    What does the first saying mean?
That despite all that happens around thee,
    Thou art the guest of the Most High.

God is in thee – with all His power,
    As the guest of thy heart;
He carries with thee on thy life's path
    What thou must carry.

XLIV

World history – perhaps you are happy
When you read about ancestors and heroic deeds;
But the enigma that everyone believes
That he alone is I – this you have not resolved.

There are many questions over which
One racks one's brains day and night.
But the question of why there must be an "I" –
Whatever one may think, one never asks.

Whatever you are, whatever you must live,
You have willed it within All-Possibility.

XLV

Late summer has now kissed the land;
With weary rustling in the woods;
The little flowers on the hill
Bow their heads towards autumn.
The rose glows in the evening light,
And fades away – spring is long past;
A man stands there and, quite alone,
Harkens to the Creator's song.

This poem – not the last two lines –
I wrote as a child almost eighty years ago.
When I was a child, I wanted to be a poet –
God can also reveal Himself in little flowers.

XLVI

There is not only the beauty of becoming,
There is also that of contemplative un-becoming —
Thus the extinction that beautifies the soul,
When it leans upon the Good of all Goods.

When thoughts flee into non-existence —
"This is the city of Benares, that I am."

XLVII

Mongols love flowers and mysteries.
The magical charm of Yellow women
Is explained by this noble pattern of soul —
With flowers one can build bridges to Heaven.

The content of the most profound questions,
The Yellow man can say with flowers.

XLVIII

First I mention Existence; without it
There would be neither space nor time.
Within these two is matter, and with it energy:
Thou canst not separate consciousness from life;
Then come also what one calls quality and quantity;
And above all of this, the human spirit is enthroned.

Wisdom is the possibility of the Spirit:
The meaning of the One and of Eternity.

XLIX

Gigantic suns journey through the night —
But they did not receive the Spirit.
On the other hand, on a very tiny planet,
There are men — sages, saints, and prophets.

L

I was not created for the earth —
Rather, the earth was created for my soul;
So that, in limitless space,
There might be a place for God's Spirit and gifts.

Man is free, and God's grace watches
Over thy world, at the God-given hearth.

LI

Thou canst be dissatisfied with thyself,
Whether it be thy fault or not;
Refuge in God — it is always open to thee,
It lightens the weight of existence.

So stand before God, whatever this world may be.

LII

Nudity is sacred through the likeness
God gave to man; worldliness, however,
Desecrates the body. Inversely, clothing
Often means the evil one's hatred of the sacred.

The gods, it is said, rejoice over the body,
For Lakshmī dwells in every noble woman
And blesses the surrounding world. India loves Nature:
Beauty and freedom in the wake of the gods.

LIII

In recent times, the godlike dances
Of the *devadassis* in temples and at festivals
Were harshly forbidden; customs
And feelings had become superficial and coarse.
The sacred is burden for the evil one –
To him, beauty and truth are equally hateful.

Nonetheless, the Spirit's messengers keep faithful watch.

LIV

One should know, whether one wants to or not,
That, in the present-day world, there is a devil's net
That seeks to corrupt everything; so beware –
And may God free thee from this work of deceit.
Do not take pleasure in dismal events;
But nevertheless, always be conscious of the danger.

LV

In good times, there were also dark clouds –
And in difficult times, there are rays of light.
For everywhere there are men of God,
Who prepare the way for Light's victory.

LVI

The spiritual life has two dimensions:
Emptiness for God and contemplation of the nobly beautiful.
Vacare Deo, then the way of *darshan* –
A noble longing for Paradise
That interiorizes us, and not passion,
Which has nothing to do with the Spirit's power.
The *sannyasi* flees the snares of life –
But Abhinavagupta sees the ray from the Divine
In the noble things on earth.

"God is the Outward and the Inward," says
The Word which transcends all illusion.

LVII

Whatever the brain may compulsively think,
Thou canst always take refuge in the One.
Whatever these times may be, thou needst not grieve,
So long as God's Name is near.

LVIII

In spring I saw a tree with blossoms
Like little lotus cups; to dwell therein
Seemed like a paradise to me.
So it must be above, where dwell the angels of God.

Thou art in thy lotus, if thou
Rememb'rest God – here and with fervor.

LIX

Three main thoughts are beloved by the dervish:
He thinks of God, to Whom worship is due;
Then of the Prophet, whom he piously greets;
And finally of himself: may God forgive!

LX

In every faith, there blooms the wreath of roses.
Who was first to find the rosary?
Doubtless India: *Brahma Satyam.* — Everywhere
The rosary sustains the litany in holy hours.

The litany: words that fell from Heaven
To lead the soul to the goal of existence.

LXI

How curious to be a creature who very soon
Will be swept away like withering leaves by the wild wind,
Yet on the other hand, with God's power and grace,
Will remain in heavenly immortality.

Mystery of light become dust —
Thou, O man, art a totality or nothing.

LXII

In God there is no sorrow –
This thou must understand well;
Think that the Lord is the Highest Good,
And let illusion vanish.

The earthly world is impermanent;
Patience – this is one thing;
Then faith – so that in thy heart
The solace of Eternity may shine.

Peace that overcomes the soul –
See how it lies within thy hand.

LXIII

Necessity is beyond all limitations –
Over mere possibility thou shouldst not grieve.
Bring back thy "perhaps" to the necessary;
Necessary is Truth – and its happiness.

LXIV

The best consolation is spiritual duty:
Man should not be ashamed of giving
When he gives what the Lord bestowed on him –
To give, it is said, is more blessed than to receive.

The deepest consolation is God –
In Pure Being alone dost thou find God's final Word.

LXV

The snuffer and the flint — two symbols
Of the wisdom that hushes the noise of the soul,
Or, inversely, kindles the Spirit;
In both, the soul's delusion is combatted.

The snuffer's meaning: to vanish like the day;
The flint means: to come into being like the morning.
In every attitude that bears witness to the True,
The Highest Good is hidden.

Vacare Deo — the silence of all stirrings;
The tendency towards God — "I love because I love."

LXVI

Faith is holding fast to God's Truth;
In this sense, it is immutable
Like Truth itself. But faith is
Also life in the deepest folds of the heart:
It is a union with what the Message offers
And with what the believer guards in his heart —

The mystery of the powers that transform us.

LXVII

Music, someone thought, should lift us up to Heaven,
As every church hymn seeks to do;
However the prolonged chanting of monks
Is not always more profound than Solveig's song.
The magic lies in the inherent worth of the melody,
And not merely in the song's intention.

In what way is music rooted in the Divine?
Ask not about the geometry of wine,
Nor where Eden's Garden is located —
Music is like the beatific radiance of Being.

LXVIII

The pious Moslem is averse to music,
Because it does not stimulate the soul to virtue;
Not so the dervish, who is partial to music,
Because it awakens in his heart the love of God.

LXIX

Man's strength bears witness to God's power;
A beautiful woman bears witness to God's love.
God's Being shines in the spirit of both:
It is the Spirit that creates the one human being.

LXX

Warlike people want to have a king
Who is in keeping with their violent nature;
However, one wants to pacify one's conscience,
So, if one kills, one does it with a heavenward intention —
But enough. This is human history —
May God give us serenity above such delusion!

True, the world often needs fight and victories —
But not a field of ruins that smolders all too long.
Certainly, our time is not better —

And all times flow toward the Judgment.

LXXI

The cult of the goddess is alien to the Semites,
So God sent them Mary, ever helpful
And near to man. Her image — a star —
Shines at the edge of the ocean, early and late:
A greeting and a grace from the Kingdom of God —
A sign for us that stands in the sky.

LXXII

The inward "yes" to God is timeless like Eternity.
I know not who I am;
I only want to know that the One is —
And that He timelessly remains in my mind.

LXXIII

There are three miracles on this grain of sand that is the earth:
Consciousness, then reason, then Intellect —
Wisdom and holiness. And may God grant
That our heart be the seat of the True.

LXXIV

Seeing — our response to light;
Hearing — our opening to sound.
Luminosity that breaks through the deep night —
Sonority that enters the depth of the heart.

Both are united in dance with song;
See how the Divine speaks in symbols.

LXXV

Certitude of salvation requires the best act of the heart,
Accompanied by nobility of soul:
Humility and generosity. Blessèd the man
To whom God has given the grace of virtue.

Certitude of the Lord is unconditional;
Certitude of salvation is a conditional star.

LXXVI

Serene "no," and holy "yes":
"No" to doubt, supposition, and verbosity;
"Yes" to God's truth and presence —
To the liberating awakening of thy soul.

LXXVII

In society, whether he wishes to or not,
Man must have the courage sometimes to say no —
Without fearing what others think;
One cannot always please others.

Among people, one must stand upright —
Many an annoyance will be swept away by the wind.

LXXVIII

In life, childhood is unique,
But one does not know it; one cannot know it.
Old age too is unique —
But one knows it, and one suffers from the fissures
Of the last days.
It is different with youth:
It almost seems to be without beginning, without end;
Then comes the time of maturity, and thou feelest
The slow approach of a great change.

LXXIX

In the space of the universe thousands upon thousands of suns
Are moving, and one day they too will disappear;
Space, and with it time, will be cold and empty.

If God so wills, there will be a return.
Say not that what is precious is reduced to nothing –
It is preserved in the Highest Good.

"To be or not to be, that is now the question."
God brings the splendor of the good to light –
Let us praise the thousand wonders of the Creator.

LXXX

"Heaven helps those who help themselves" –
This is will-power. – Then resignation:
"Man proposes, and God disposes" – this thou must accept.
Let the world have its play of possibilities.

Patience and fervor. Without this equilibrium,
Thou canst not obtain the good goal.

LXXXI

Man and his destiny – two different things.
Thou see'st the man, as he stands before thee;
Thou see'st his face, but not his *karma* –
Thou see'st not how he walks into the future.

Live in God, and trust in Providence –
And listen to what God speaks in thy heart.

LXXXII

Thou shouldst not despair because of man's foolishness;
Thou must take people as they are.
The fact that, despite all troubles, thou art full of hope,
Does not mean that thou art blind to illusion and nonsense.

Remain before the world what thou art in thy spirit;
Just as God always is what He is.

LXXXIII

The Lord's Prayer, the *Fātiha*, and the *Shemā*
Correspond to Names of God.
They are revealed frameworks
Of what God has to say about Himself.

On the other hand, the syllable *Om* contains
The river of the whole Vedic revelation.

LXXXIV

Believers are always in a good state,
Said the Messenger of God; for they dwell
In resignation, close to humility, and in trust;
The Lord will reward them.

Patience and trust proclaim God's grace
And unite truth and beauty in the depth of the heart.

In every stroke of fate, be serene —
For the trial's severity also has some good in it.

LXXXV

Thunder, lightning, and storm — God can be all of this,
Even though He is Peace and gentle breeze;
In the high Presence of thy Lord,
Thou feelest the grace-filled fragrance of Peace.
Love of God is not without fear of God —
Never forget this midst the stirrings of thy soul.

He who seeks God's grace, knows love;
And fear brings forth the fruit of self-knowledge.

LXXXVI

In life, thou must often see what is ugly —
Which does not mean that thou must be ugly thyself;
So let things be, and go thy way —
Time wil, in any case, blow away the nightmare.

LXXXVII

Passion equals prejudice and injustice;
So remember well:
Playing with truth is not a joke —
It is not a viaticum for eternity.

LXXXVIII

What the soul of man deeply contemplates,
That it will become. There is much that is beautiful on earth;
If thou dost contemplate it with the gaze of thy heart,
Then thy heart's core will itself become beauty.

Look at the true, which within beauty, makes thee happy —
And at the beautiful that dwells within the true.

LXXXIX

What is the meaning of princely palaces,
With their pomps, festivals,
Musicians, and naked dancing girls?
It is to bring a paradise into our world.
Perhaps a two-edged sword; not to be condemned,
For it can bring good tidings,
If we are not foolish.
Let a ray
From Heaven enter into our poverty.

Hagar Firdaus bar ruye zamīn ast,
Hamīn ast u-hamīn ast u-hamīn ast.

XC

One of the most miserable things I know
Is a bad imitation of paradise —
Such is the baroque. I prefer
The meanest hut in the smallest meadow.

XCI

Object and point of view — the first is the thing in itself,
And the second, what things are for me;
For what counts is not just how I see things,
But also my position when I look at them.

Every religion has its meaning,
And points to the One Most High.
In all forms of the Spirit, in all religions,
Dwells but one Truth, which will reward you:

There is, determining everything, God Most High;
And then, following His will, comes the neighbor.

XCII

Thou shouldst not stubbornly insist on this or that,
Trying to force the world's absurdity to be logical;
The wise man, who sees through the world,
Will not begrudge the play of All-Possibility.

So be not impatient like a child,
And let things be what they are.
Be content with thy destiny,
And be full of hope, for thou art in God's Hands.

XCIII

First comes Truth; but we also need
Combat and love: defense of the good,
And, on the other hand, the propagation
Of mankind itself — under the Lord's banner.
The sage practices prayer and meditation;
The hero battles, and he loves woman.

The warrior's nature is not combat alone,
But also magnanimity; and the lover
Does not merely enjoy, he also must honor woman;
Only under these conditions are combat and love pure.

XCIV

Dieu premier servi — thus spake the noble virgin of Orleans;
Then, and on the basis of this maxim,
She thought, come the duties that we must
Faithfully perform for God and our neighbor.
The duties: first the great, and then the small;
The starting-point is always the Most High.

XCV

Just as a ship plows through the dark ocean,
The Remembrance of God penetrates our life,
Be it quiet or stormy; our existential path
Would be nothing if it did not tend towards God.

XCVI

Reality is everything — appearance very little;
The Intellect[1] is both, and is King of existence.
Reality, appearance, and Intellect: this is the great doctrine —
God grant that the soul may turn Inward.

Where the alchemy of the Veda blossoms,
There is Selfhood — *Aham Brahmāsmi*.

XCVII

What does it mean that Thy Name is holy?
It means that It brings silence —
Vacare Deo: the noisy illusion
Of world and soul sinks into nothingness before God.

Sanctificetur Nomen Tuum. It is God
Alone who resounds in holy silence.

XCVIII

It cannot be otherwise: wherever light
Breaks through the blackness of a spiritual night,
The evil one has something to say —
He cannot gain victory, but he can torment thee.

For good men, to struggle is a duty;
Another duty is to endure evil.

XCIX

Firstly, there is the "no" that liberates thee;
Secondly, there is a good, strong "yes":
The "no" to a thinking that is of no avail;
The "yes" to God – His solace is always there.

The One and All, He supports the soul –
Much may be far away, but thy Shepherd is nigh.

C

"Man shall not live by bread alone,
But by every word of God" –
God gives me His Word, that it may be
My happiness, and my heart's refuge.

God pronounces His Word – then it must enter me,
And remain in my heart.

CI

What a miracle it is that flowers have a scent –
It is the same with souls that are filled with God;
This is the spiritual power or *baraka*
Of which pious witnesses speak –
Or perhaps you have felt it yourselves,
In a soul that has become the bride of Truth.

CII

Peace of soul I owe to the Lord –
Who is the Serene and the Eternally True.
I also owe it to myself – for it is not admissible
That I spoil the kernel of His creation.

Truth and Beauty have united
To manifest God and His peace.

CIII

In the *'Isāwa* Order, Shaikh Ahmad learned
How to charm snakes; then a Shaikh from the *Darqāwa* Order
Came to him and said: "Follow me –
Henceforth thou must listen to a better message:
Take thy flute, and learn to charm the soul.
A wiser thing thou canst not do."

What is this flute? Not a weak reed, but
The Name of God at the door of Heaven.

CIV

It is not easy to swim against the current –
But man must do so in the turmoil of the world;
He can do it with a miraculous power
Come from above – this is the love of God.

CV

It was at my high school[2] in Basle: I said to my
Classmates: "On Christmas Day 1932
Let us all meet at the Cathedral Pfalz;
In the meantime, let us work hard."

In the aforesaid year, I was with the Shaikh –
And was received into his Order.
On Christmas Day, I walked along the shore,
And, not without longing, I looked toward the north.

It was not lack of gratitude for Heaven's gift –
But a man likes to have a homeland.

CVI

The poems may seem very unequal;
They deal with the great, and also with the small:
With what is seen by the eye of thy heart –
And with what happens in the outside world.

The soul can look in all directions –
Even with the small, it can build bridges
From "here" to "there"; from things that happen
To words that are inscribed in God.

CVII

Where can we find rest, it may be asked –
Rest in Rest Itself, the spirit would tell us.
Understand well: what man lacks,
God has provided for him within the world itself.

Thou mayest complain: I am only an "I".
Be what thou art in God: thy deepest being.

CVIII

The Scots dance between eggs placed on the floor;
This is what the sage does when he expounds the deepest truths –
When he speaks of what is foreign to everyday thought –
And for which human language has no words.

CIX

Above all, man must be reasonable;
Be neither angry nor saddened over vain, worldly concerns;
The more reasonable thou art,
The more Heaven will bring thee consolation.

CX

First comes the Intellect, and then reason;
You will find both in the guild of the wise.
For, on the basis of what is true in God,
Earthly things are clear to reason.

CXI

Perhaps there is a shadow in the soul –
Whence does it come? It may lie in existence itself;
Let this suffice thee. For God is God;
Thou shouldst not blame what He created.

On this earth, evil is near;
Wert thou in Heaven, there would be no shadow.

CXII

The poor man has not much to lose —
His life may be difficult, but his death is easy.
Belongings have value, if one is poor in one's heart:
The spiritually poor, whether wealthy or not,
Can, with God's help, attain the Highest Good.

CXIII

Reality, Truth, Intellect — these are the highest values;
Then come strength and generosity; and, on the other hand,
Beauty and love. See how God
Communicates His own Being to the world and to men.

All this is Divinity; or Its ray —
Its luminous trace in human nature.

CXIV

The bride adorned in her jewelry — a *mu'allim* said —
Is more beautiful than the nakedness of her body;
This is how dour theologians misunderstand
The God-willed splendor of woman —
It is as if the Lord did not know the value of His creation.

In the case of all appearances, including beautiful women,
One must always look at the nature of things.

CXV

Be not depressed because people come to thee
To ask questions; be happy
That thou canst help. If people's burdens are
Especially heavy — thou shouldst welcome it all the more.

CXVI

All too often people ask: why?
God knows well the answer; ye need not know everything.
What cannot not be, must be;
And what cannot be straight, is crooked.

Who wove *Māyā*'s iridescent gown?
Existence and non-existence are in God's hands.

CXVII

It can happen that one is angry with someone —
And that one is angry because of being angered;
If one does not know clearly where to turn,
Prayer for the person should be the solution.

CXVIII

The end — it is said — justifies the means;
On condition that the end be good,
And that the means not be vile —
False and despicable like the devil's guile.

No good man will kill for the sake of killing
And redden the earth with just men's blood.
Certainly one must kill in order to survive,
And to protect those who strive toward the Truth.

CXIX

An animal is beautiful if it belongs to a noble species –
And man is beautiful if God gives him beauty;
The animal is fragment, but man is totality –
See how the Lord has fashioned the nature of man.

Say not that the animal has nothing in common with man –
Into the noble animal enters many a blessing.

CXX

How can man pray for something
When resignation to God's decree
Is said to be the highest virtue?
Do not forget: petition is obedience.

Petitioning God and accepting one's destiny –
Both are Scriptural. Hope and patience –
Both must be profoundly present in our faith.

CXXII

Bali has been called "the island of the gods" –
Here India blossoms amongst beautiful Yellow people,
In the midst of a dark blue sea;
It is a golden land of childlike love of the gods –
Where however, from time to time, the mountains tremble –
Paradises like this must exist.

CXXIII

Sometimes, when air and clouds are favorable,
The whole landscape, at sunset, is enveloped
In a golden mist. The world becomes cool –
And the evening wind dreams of the fragrance of roses.

See how the evening provides a symbol
Of God's grace gilding thy soul.

CXXIV

When worldly people go carousing,
I would like to interrupt their din –
With what? The everyday life of fools is quite loud.

I would like to speak of the silence of God.
For silence is a special sound –
It is an opening to the Song of Heaven;

This reminds me of Shankara's words:
The cessation of all mental agitation
Is like the city of Benares –which I am.

CXXV

There are many men who wish to be a father,
And many women who wish to be a mother.
But others have a different vocation in mind –
They want to live with the Lord alone.

There must be both kinds of men,
And thou see'st both kinds throughout the world.
Everyone should follow his essential nature –
And, in his own way, do what pleases the Lord.

CXXVI

It may be good to bring a child into the world,
And to educate him with love and care —
But when he grows up, the world will take the trouble
To do the opposite: to draw the child's soul,
Which is still wavering, into the realm of deception.

Therefore, give the child a right soul at an early age,
So that, with courage, he may choose the True.

CXXVII

There is a God, who dwells high in Heaven;
Who is good and mighty, and who created
The world and all that it contains;
Who rewards good souls in Paradise,
And severely punishes the bad.
To Him, who rules over all things,
Let us pray faithfully day by day.

This you must teach to your dear little ones —
And attach them at an early age to the Sovereign Good.

CXXVIII

Peace treaties cause new wars;
Why? Because in making them one forgets the people,
Who are innocent of the actions of their leaders.

One should not punish a whole people with one's victory.
One punishes oneself by not wishing to see
That, in one's triumph, a new calamity growls.

Objection: were not the people previously enthusiastic?
Yes indeed — but their soul had been poisoned.
It is no joke to sit in judgment —

But I sometimes think about world history.

CXXIX

A sense of duty has often impelled me
To bring to light of day things that are not beautiful —
We cannot, even if we would rather,
Always flee the dark side of the true.

CXXX

The condition of divine promises
Is always just conformity on the part of man;
Because there is no divine promise for one
Whose heart is not in accord with God.

St. Bernard's crusade could not succeed
With knights who followed their robbers' lust;
In short, if it seems that God did not speak truly,
It is because man has broken his word.

God says: "I give you my Compassion";
It is implicit: "If ye be pure."

CXXXI

The naked Lallā shunned the illusion
Of the earthly dream; faithful to the deepest Truth,
She wished herself to be the True, even before the world –
Because only from the Truth comes the goodness of man.

The same mystery can be found in other lands:
Men have wished, free from empty everyday illusion,
To dwell blissfully in the house of Pure Selfhood.

CXXXII

Emptiness for God and trust in God
Are like two hands clasping the same jewel.
Thou shouldst let the One Divinity act
In the activity of thy heart.

Songs without Names

Twelfth Collection

The sun lovingly gives us light and warmth;
And God, from his Pure Being, gives us truth and love.
Thou wast created in God's image –
So thou too must give to others from what God has given thee;
And what thou givest, thou must above all be

Songs without Names

Twelfth Collection

I

Everything in life is a constant going –
There is no standstill; life is movement.
Whether thou wishest it or not – there is one goal;
And if thou art wise, thou goest toward God.

II

Emptiness for God, and trust in Him,
Are like two hands holding
The same jewel: our divine goal –
And may God transform our heart to light.

"And when ye sacrifice, do so with joy –
Let not the left hand know what the right hand doeth."
What this means, reason can tell us:
In this case, only one hand is acting.

III

Prayer is timeless, as is the Most High:
Devotion is to stand eternally before the One.
But we are temporal, so prayer is as the same time
A movement – a movement towards God.

IV

As a child, I was not really obedient;
Why? Because I loved my duty.
So my parents did not seek to give me orders –
They could count on the child's understanding.

Why do I say this? Not to praise myself,
But to offer something consoling –
To approve attitudes that are proper.

V

My way was ambivalent — much went wrong,
But things became better with the years;
Finally the difficulties faded away.
And, *Deo gratias*, the work succeeded.

VI

One might think that concentration on the One
Is as an impoverishment; one would thereby forget
That this One is also infinite —
And that out of It flows the Divine Mercy.

VII

Well-intentioned reserve is a virtue —
One should not give one's heart to just anyone.
Certainly, one must respect the pious and the noble —
But it should be indifferent what others think of thee.

VIII

It is a sin against the Holy Spirit,
Not to protect the Most High within our heart
From false tendencies in our soul: and not to use
The door towards Him that He has offered to us.

According to St. James, whoever knows how to do good,
And does not do it, commits a sin — and cannot rest in God.

IX

Sacred art is not always good:
It often represents a people's piety
And simpleness. A truly holy image
Bears witness to the profound splendor of Heaven.

X

Man can be intelligent or not; with this
Comes a third element: the wind
Of the soul's delusion. Intelligent or stupid,
Man becomes deaf and blind through the poison of error.

Beware, O friend of God, of psychoses —
Be faithful to the Lord. "Patience brings roses."

XI

Back-biting is an evil thing;
To defend the bad, because one considers
This to be a work of virtue, is just as ugly;
Only veracity is indispensable.

Errors — which poison — must be recognized;
Otherwise one can no longer distinguish good from evil.

XII

Even when God threatens, a reservation
Is implied: if the people improve,
The punishment is withdrawn. This in no way
Diminishes the seriousness of the threat.

So it was in Nineveh. The people donned
Sackcloth and ashes, and the threat was withdrawn –
But Jonah did not understand; be that as it may –
Man is free; and God does what He will.

XIII

Jonah wanted to know something better –
He had to pay for this in the belly of a whale.
What does this mean? That between two spiritual degrees,
There is a night in which we must call upon God.
The Lord hears us, and sends us the shining day –
The freedom that lay hidden in ourselves.

XIV

Spiritual nudity and spiritual wine –
Mysteries of Noah, maker of the ark;
Woe to the fools who did not understand him –
Who laughed at the prophet's strange message.

XV

Formerly it was thought that one and one are two –
Today people think this is far too simple.
They take seriously only what is neither straight nor crooked;
But towards the True, they remain silent.

The Essential is always clear and sharp,
And satisfies the fundamental need of our Intellect;
What is offered us at the tavern of fools?
The intoxication of pride – a poisonous mixed drink.

XVI

Prophets, saints, and sages:
The prophet brings a form of faith – a religion;
The saint lives it; the sage opens
A luminous realm of Pure Spirit
Beyond form. Prophets are also wise men,
Yet about the highest Truth they speak softly;
To the sage, holiness bestows light.

God and our heart are united in eternity.

XVII

As seen starting from the ego, God is an object –
He is the One Being, the absolutely Other;
As seen by the Divine Self, I am a mere thing,
Not a consciousness that can observe the world.

And yet I am within God's Being – and He
Is reality within my very core;
Without God's Selfhood, my ego would be nothing –

The Lord is the source of primordial substance and of light.

XVIII

Auctoritas – teaching authority counts
Only in pure metaphysics, not in cosmology,
Which is always fluctuating;
Shankara is an infallible shield
Only when he speaks as a master of Advaita –
And not on the basis of the Sānkhya theory,
Which only has to do with the description of things.

Fidelity to literalness is hardly a guarantee;
Infallibility belongs to a deeper level.

XIX

In my childhood, I was obliged to dissimulate;
The adult world did not understand me. Why?
Because I bore within myself the kernel of wisdom –
And this was vexing to others.

It was not wanted; so I feigned dullness,
And it made me ill. But Truth must always conquer –
What God has given us, can never fail.

XX

If one does not recognize the work of a sage,
It is firstly because one hates the Truth;
And then because of jealousy: the value of a great Spirit
Is a burden for small-minded, ambitious spirits.

Not everyone who brings the Truth is great;
Great is the True that his spirit has grasped.

XXI

Intelligence and will-power, humility and goodness —
These are the God-willed values of man.
And what of genius, it might be asked?
Even the devil's brother can be a genius.

It is often said that some saints were naïve —
But for many a man, it would have been better
Had he been healed of the poison of his genius —
So that his soul could swim in quiet waters.

XXII

There are three degrees of consciousness:
Firstly, we are always conscious of earthly things;
Then, with the spirit that measures, we distinguish
Between the Essential and the non-essential.
And thirdly, the Intellect understands
What the deepest meaning of existence evokes:
The Highest Reality — the Divine Power,
Which towers above all, and creates all.

Abide in the house of the Highest Wisdom —
Consciousness of the Absolute makes a man.

XXIII

Thou hast a house, meadows, and a forest —
At every moment, thou canst think of the Lord;
And therewith thou hast eternal ownership —
All the rest, thou canst give away to the world.

XXIV

Jesus said: it is easier for a camel
To force itself through the eye of a needle,
Than for a fool to gain the kingdom of Heaven –
A rich man, attached to his property.

XXV

A consolation when in need: Truth, and trust in God.
The truth that God is Absolute Reality,
The Highest Good; and trust that knows
That the All-Powerful will look upon our need –

He, who forgives the weakness of the believer.

XXVI

Om, bhūr bhuvah svah –
Tat Savitur varenyam.
"Earth and air, then heavenly expanse –
God Savitā, who came to enlighten us"
With His eternal Word – *Brahma satyam.*

So says the Gāyatrī. First, the three worlds –
Within them, the ray of grace from the Divinity,
So that liberation may be our destiny.

XXVII

In the Gospel, it is written: Knock and –
It shall be opened unto you;
If ye want bread, and your heart is pure,
The Lord will not give you a stone.
He who asks with faith shall receive mercy –
So take refuge in patience.
It is faith that can move mountains –
If ye love God.

XXVIII

In the Sāvitrī it is said: Earth, wind,
And heavenly expanse; may Savitā
Grant us enlightenment, God's gift,
Which from above flows down to earth.

Bhūr bhuvah svah: earth is matter;
Air or wind is the psyche, the world of the soul;
Heaven is the Spirit; Savitâ is
The divine ray that descends into the darkness.

The Names of God penetrate the spheres
Of cosmic unfolding; even in the world of matter,
Thou canst hear the eternal Words of the Divinity.

XXIX

Do not believe, O man, that thou belongest to thyself –
For thou belongest to thy Creator. Whatever thou doest
In thy life should not be haphazard –
So do whatever thou must do through God.

Freedom is not the sense of well-being of the fool –
Freedom is happiness in what Allah wills.

XXX

The first consolation is God's Reality;
The second is thy Lord's Compassion.
Then the accomplishment of thy life's duty —
And others too; but there are none better.

XXXI

It is strange how venerable ancient cultures
Suddenly collapse — end of the story.
How is this possible? Because, in a world
Of foolishness, men who are too far removed
From their traditional origins, become tired of their dignity.
A sanctuary that suddenly falls into ruin —
A beautiful myth that fades into nothingness.

XXXII

Neither space nor time can expand,
Nor can any thing or event grow indefinitely;
But they repeat themselves,
As is required by infinity.

Space and time: existence and energy,
Rays of Pure Being. Form and number:
They make our world, only God knows how —
His is the creative Power, His is the choice.

XXXIII

For the *pneumatic*,[1] the center is
The Pure Intellect — not the empirical ego;
The *psychic*, on the other hand,
Knows only himself as the center of knowledge.
Then comes the *hylic*: drunk with pleasures,
And deeply sunk in the illusion of matter.

Yet man is not incurably closed —
How many souls have been transmuted!

XXXIV

Attachment to people and things,
Given by our surroundings, is the aura,
Indeed the substance, of our soul;
It constitutes our ego, and one's whole life.

Yet it is little, yea, a nothingness, before God.
He gave us the right to be ourselves;
But, on the other hand, we are his property —
For in prayer, I am alone with God.

In Heaven too, we shall have neighbors;
And what we love, we have in the Most High.
In Heaven there are no passions —
Yet something of the earth remains in us.

Even the greatest friend of God possesses an ego —
In our deepest self, we are united with God.

XXXV

I am neither Moslem, Jew, nor Christian;
I am the gust of wind that trembles in God –
The Spirit that dwells everywhere and nowhere;
So said a Sufi, who lived within Islam.

Jesus said: the wind – thou knowest not how it blows;
And so it is with the soul that has been chosen –
With him who is born of the Holy Spirit.

The call from God to God, that never fades away.

XXXVI

One could describe Paradise as a circle
In whose center radiates God's Presence;
The circle turns, like an immense wheel –
Like the ring of *gopis* gathered round Shrī Krishna.

A circle that bows down before God's Presence –
And also rises in a drunken dance;
The Presence of God is the axis which,
Like a tree-trunk bearing the wind-tossed crown,
Shapes the melody of the kingdom of Heaven.

XXXVII

God is the Inward, for one does not see Him;
He is the Outward, for He manifests Himself
In the Universe, as well as in His heavenly Kingdom –
Hence Dante's poem speaks of the blessèd in Paradise.
And the pious who go to the place of salvation –
Which of them would not wish to see the Prophets there?

In Heaven there is the vision of God,
But not everything can be seen by the souls.
When God manifests His unique Being in us,
Then our ego, of necessity, disappears.

Man must experience both the inward and the outward
If his spirit wants to ascend to Pure Being.

XXXVIII

Shankara's Vedanta, and with it, *japa-yoga* –
In wisdom, this is the path of paths.
Firstly, discernment, then the soul's abiding
In That which is: *Ātmā*, beyond *Māyā*.

XXXIX

The sage has no home – it may be
That Shankara and Lallā were constant wayfarers
Because their home was everywhere and nowhere –
Because their home was deep within their heart.

XL

The Idea is true to itself and pure;
But what is clad in form is fragile;
Where there is form, there is the world's din;
The Spirit is faithful, the formal corruptible.

Form is the garment of a possibility;
To say form is to say limit and opposition.
The husk can bear witness, it can also corrupt –
It is ready for any betrayal.

XLI

Languages that have dignity are fragile –
Thus it is with German, which carries
Within itself the Bible; this the noble person loves –
But the undignified man is corruptible.

Modern Germans have but one dream:
To wreak vengeance on their ancient language.
They have room in their heads for only one thing:
The shallow gibberish of newspapers.

Do not let yourselves be robbed of your language;
By corrupting words, one murders the soul.

XLII

Worldly culture — an empty waste
And futile pursuit; when the storm has died,
The broom of time will sweep away
All delusion like autumn leaves.

Consider the wise economy of nature;
Each year brings forth new wonders
In God's language, not man's compulsions.
Richness in poverty — simple and marvelous.

Not that we should despise man's work
When, arising from the True, it ennobles him;
Let us look on man's work in the light of God.

XLIII

A Greek monk told me: "Under the Turks,
The life of our monasteries was not disturbed:
But the moment we were liberated from the Turkish yoke,
Hundreds of monasteries were closed by the Greeks."

A sign of our enlightened time.

XLIV

Poems must offer a variety of things —
Whether one wishes to or not, one has to teach,
Because the world is the world, be it great or small —
Thou canst not always sing of the good.
And may God forgive thy to-and-fro —
True words, thou needst not regret.

XLV

The lark cannot rise higher and higher –
After its flight, it will rest a little.
Its home is indeed the vault of heaven –
It has another home on green branches.

With the soul of man, it is the same image –
Everything has its season. The Lord is indulgent.

XLVI

Divine Grace comes, a gentle miracle –
Like a mild and cool spring breeze
In burning sunshine; like the murmuring of a fountain,
Whose freshness flows through the parched soul.

When the soul, moved inwardly by God,
Remembers Him alone.

XLVII

North, South, East, West – home is indeed the best.
Doesn't this rhyme have a deeper meaning?
In thy heart is thy true home –
For God's presence blooms therein.

XLVIII

God is Peace. And the evil one wants
To destroy the peace in our soul.
If thou livest and reposest in Eternal Peace,
Satan can hiss, but can achieve nothing.

XLIX

Peace — Pure Being; the equilibrium
Of the innumerable possibilities of *Ātmā*.
All in One; One in All.
See how all creatures are united in God.

L

The spoken word — does something remain
With the person who spoke it? No, but also yes.
If the word manifests our essence,
Then yes; if not, then nothing remains.

LI

The word; the intention. A word in itself is a form;
Intention gives it life. Distinguish between words
Which mean just anything and others which,
With a right intention, can save us —
Names of the Divinity and of the saints.

God's Word will purify us from evil —
But our intention must piously participate.

LII

White and black: they abruptly contradict each other,
Just as differences break through pure light; day and night.
Red and white: life's blood, and the harsh ice of purity.
A similar opposition: black and red:
Red is life, black is somber death.
Then blue and yellow: blue is contemplation,
And yellow is joy — wine, woman, and song.
White and red: purity and passion;
Green and red: coolness and vital energy;
Violet and orange: sorrow and pleasure.

All this the earthly man harbors in his breast.
Look at the changing face of man —
Our soul too is refracted light.

LIII

Abstractly we understand what evil is;
All-Possibility — one must let it weave.
But concretely — when one looks at the world,
One can barely understand the existence of evil.

The reason why we are blind in this respect
Is doubtless because we are the children of Heaven.

LIV

Eternal return — there is something in this idea:
What is in time, must repeat itself;
But not the modality, not the where and why —
Human history is never plagiarized.

Similar things repeat themselves a thousand times,
But always differently. Look at the spiral of time —
It rises and falls. In every cycle of humanity
There are seasons — life is a rhythm.

LV

Greatness is not only the creation of great works —
Greatness can also be one's attitude towards life
On the basis of the Great Spirit, along with strength
And nobility — and with no other ambition
Than to live in never-changing virgin Nature,
In the wake of our ancestors.

LVI

In false language usage, greatness is merely quantity,
Outward success and appearance, "much ado about nothing";
Lacking foundation in the nature of things —
It is not noble breadth, but miserable narrowness.

In a world where everything is but appearance,
One calls great men small, and small men great.

LVII

Nobility of soul excludes curiosity;
What does not concern thee, thou shouldst not wish to know.
Everyday life is made up of many things —
Knowledge of trivialities should not concern thee.

LVIII

Truth and beauty are the two values
From which all life's happiness is made,
And God's favor. So in thy soul
Be mindful of both — of the meaning of existence.

LIX

Man is activity — for he must do something;
He is also faith — for he must believe something.
So perform the highest work and believe in it —
Then God will permit thee to be human.

LX

Truth and duty are of a masculine nature;
Beauty and love I would call feminine.
But man and woman are one in their human nature;
So both must recognize within themselves
Truth and duty, beauty and love, as their very Being.

LXI

Devotion and fervor — what magic lies
In these words! Devotion in height,
And fervor in depth: the presence
Of the True, which conquers the world within ourselves.

Devotion: a motionless light in a sanctuary;
Fervor: an inexhaustible flowing towards God.

LXII

The ego and destiny — two different things;
Thou, O man, must cope with both
And transmute them, and live them in God —
In God's favor is His kingdom on earth.

LXIII

Two things we desire from the Most High:
Help and enlightenment. Help in things that are
Too difficult for us; enlightenment, because our spirit
Can do nothing without a ray from God's sun.

LXIV

Access to God. Therein are two levels:
The first is that we can always pray;
The second is that Grace touches us
The moment we invoke God with all our heart.

LXV

Culture — this means that one has to know many things,
Even too many; but in order to remain true to oneself,
One would often like to forget what one has learned —
And write better and higher things in our heart.

How many things the soul must absorb,
Because destiny so wills; but look to the source
Within thee, which purifies and gives new life —
Which imbues the heart with light, yea even with God.

LXVI

The starting-point must often be a criticism —
For the false can provide a key to the true;
One can clearly see the True and the Good
When one must be angry over something bad.

We must admit it, and we do so gladly:
Even the false is good for something.

LXVII

A Word from above is intelligible to the soul
Not only through clarity of speech;
It can happen that a heavenly message
Brings us grace through pure and luminous being.

LXVIII

It was in the time of my youth —
    one wanted to make of me
A reasonable gentleman,
    involved in everyday things;
But I dreamt of India,
    of temples and dancing girls,
And brahmins
    meditating on *Om*.

The clever ones failed completely —
But *Om* graciously thought of me.

LXIX

Sincerity — the most beautiful adornment of the soul
Before God and men. It contains
Humility and generosity, wisdom and love of truth —
It is an open door to the soul's salvation.

Sinceritas — of what art thou made?
Of God's Spirit, that watches over all.

LXX

If one gives free play to thinking,
The specter of preoccupations rushes in;
One did not summon it. So turn to faith —
And see how quickly it heals the soul's illusion.

The evil one wants to show thee what oppresses thee —
The heart's faith convinces with silence.

LXXI

Upward, outward, and downward:
The soul has a threefold potential.
It is the emphasis that differentiates men;
What is harmful — the wise man burns it.

Māyā and the *gunas*, as the Hindus say —
Primordial matter must contain all possibilities.
The world is woven of qualities —
He who has understood this, looks Upward.

LXXII

See what the wide world offers man —
If only he watch over the good of his soul!
Freedom may push him to and fro —
But in One Path alone lies benediction.

LXXIII

The birds in the vast sky
Are the happiest of creatures — so may their lot
Appear to man. But happier than they
Is man himself, when he pays heed to the kernel of existence.

What then is happiness? It is a full consciousness
Of the essence of things, and not just of their existential husk —
Not what an animal might feel to be the goal of life.

For both animal and man — what is, is God's Will.

LXXIV

Faith is a wondrous inner power
Which does for us what we cannot do for ourselves.
Whoever finds himself in a arid state should force himself —
So that, God Willing, an angel will sing in his heart.

LXXV

In my youth, I felt weak —
Nonetheless I did what the world did not want.
I overcame all opposition;
I suffered — but I did what I had to do

With God's help. Boast not about thy strength —
Our victories are the works of the Most High.

LXXVI

It is astonishing what can be in a gaze –
All the nobility and depth of the soul.
Also its evil; but it can happen that the gaze
Of an insincere fool will deceive us.

Certainly, the eye is not obliged to show everything –
It can keep silent about the Lord's secrets.
A secret does not mean some idle triviality,
It means the grace that has come into one's heart.

LXXVII

Let not disquiet burn in thy soul –
Be still in the One, Who Himself is stillness.
Blessèd the man who, remembering the Lord,
Forgets himself in the happiness of remembrance.

LXXVIII

Very small things that happen around us
Can be the starting-point of a didactic poem;
Thou mayst spin thy words with small threads –
Hidden greatness thou canst not avoid.

And of little things thou needst not be ashamed;
The stuff on which the world is built, is greatness.

LXXIX

God as the Inward, as the Outward –
Maintain a balance between these two perspectives.
There are ascetics who see the inward alone –
To see God only in the outward does not exist.

LXXX

If ether were a hard mass,
And not relatively empty – it could not
Contain the sun; thus it is with the soul:
It must empty itself in order to grasp God.

Ether in its way is also a fullness;
Likewise, emptiness of soul is not nothingness –
Its ether-substance is God's holy Will.

Vacare Deo is the substance of light.

LXXXI

In space, something must be present;
In time, something must happen.
See how things are different –
How they come and fade away.

So hold fast to the One Being
Which contains every good
And is eternal – and which, wherever thou may'st be,
Enlightens thy heart.

LXXXII

In Paradise, it is said in Islam, every man
Has a thousand wives. Why does a woman
Not have a thousand husbands? The question is meaningless,
For one must look at the nature of things.

Polygamy is in the masculine nature;
Love of a single man, corresponds to woman.
In Paradise, a woman's husband has
A thousand excellences; yet he is but one man.

Around Krishna dances the ring of beautiful *gopis;*
Krishna is just one, but he is a god –
So he is wonderful a thousandfold.

Be that as it may – a man also can love one single woman,
And place her in the Highest Heaven.
And a woman too can see in different men
Something of the one, unique belovèd.

It is true that man comes first in the couple –
But each can consecrate himself completely to the Divine.

LXXXIII

Consider, O man, the rights of plants;
The world dries up without this sign from Heaven.
But since people do not respect virgin Nature,
The traces of Paradise must everywhere yield
To the world of stone and iron.

The rights of the human body: in the southern world
Nakedness is now opposed. But it is healthy,
And above all, sacred — and for this reason
It has to disappear from the earth.

In other words, in the world of progress,
Beauty is considered barbaric and shameful.
The body has not the right to breathe or radiate —
Artificiality is the victor, and is allowed to boast.

Everything turns to stone. In hot climates,
Let the poor dwell in bamboo huts!

LXXXIV

Vacare Deo and *Amor Dei* are
The two spiritual streams that flow into the One.
Without emptiness and love,
Man cannot find the Way to the Divine.

LXXXV

Something supreme that vanishes like the wind —
Deus sive natura — is not a god.
God is the One, Immutable, Being,
That stands high above all idle imaginings.

Nature is effect, it is not cause.
God is the Supreme Essence; the world is ephemeral —
A spark from the Godhead's eternal Light.

LXXXVI

Sadness comes from nature,
But the evil one always wishes to stir it up:
He, who always seeks our harm,
Wants to dislodge man's faith.

Of all the things thou hast received from God,
Faith is the one most hated by the evil one.

LXXXVII

Intelligence has two dimensions:
Discernment between Reality and appearance,
And between the essential and the merely contingent.
Be ready to distinguish
Between yes and no, black and white —
Let nothing in your minds be veiled in fog.

Thereafter comes logic, syllogism: here too
One needs first the light of discernment;
Whoever reasons without a clear starting-point,
Thinks in vain and gets nowhere —
Even though he clothe his discourse in pleasant words,
And avoids any sin against logic.

LXXXVIII

Many people like ostentation — in the kingdom of Heaven,
They want to have castles brimming
With golden ornaments and diamonds; it seems to me
That beatitude takes no pleasure in vanity —

It has nothing to do with gold and precious stones.
There would be nothing more beautiful than Paradise,
Even if it had nothing else to offer
But the splendor of flowers on an earthly meadow.

LXXXIX

Form, by definition, is static;
Unceasing self-change would be satanic.
See, this is the quintessence of the noble:
That it remain true to its divine potentiality.

Nobility of soul can be described as follows:
The soul should remain what God willed it to be.
To change oneself in a heavenly direction is no betrayal –
It is to return to what God has bestowed.

XC

Dignity is to remain faithful to the Inward –
And in the outward, not to deny the sacred
Which God has placed in our heart,
Nor assimilate the turmoil and foolishness of the world.
Dignity is to be what every man should remain
According to God's intention. Let not the evil one
Depose thee from the noble throne of the human state;
For, since the devil does not like the sacred,
He hates the door to the Divine.
What pleases God, thou shouldst inscribe in thy heart –
So fear thy Lord, and take heed
What thy soul does, and how it does it.

XCI

Matter, form, and life — and above them, knowledge;
From these man is fashioned.
And then man's likeness to God,
Through which the Lord has raised us out of nothingness.

Matter means to be "here"; and form
Means to be "thus", in a particular way.
Life animates form; and knowledge instills in man
A striving worthy of the human state.

XCII

The Koran says that men are lost —
Except those who find refuge
In God's Truth, and in patience;
See how these two graces combine —

How patience consoles thee within time;
And how, through the benevolence of the Most High,
Truth renews thy heart from out of eternity.

XCIII

Past, present, and future:
The past is origin, in the hand of the Creator;
Otherwise it is a naught,
Because it slips forever from thy "now."

The present: be conscious of thy duty;
And accept what thou must bear.

The future: be always disposed towards the True,
Just as time fills the cup of life.
Thy heart must be resigned to what is written;
But more than this: the meaning of existence is to strive

Until the Infinite satisfies thy thirst.

XCIV

Vedanta is discernment between
Reality and what is mere appearance.
No wisdom in the world can be more true
Than the *Ātmā-Māyā* relationship.

Then *japa-yoga*: the permanent concentration
On what one has recognized as real.
For what one thinks is true, one must become –
So let sacred will crown reason,

Because nothing else has meaning here on earth.

XCV

Māyā is of two kinds: it is the manifestation of *Ātmā* –
In this sense, *Māyā* is *Ātmā*'s form –
Or it is merely illusion, pure nothingness.
In both cases, *Ātmā* is the norm.

"Everything is *Ātmā*" – all that exists;
Ātmā which, as Being, flows into the naught.

XCVI

Certitude of God, accompanied by resignation and trust.
Do not torment thyself with too much thinking –
In this world of absurdities,
God will give thee anew Truth and Peace.

XCVII

Contradiction often lies in the nature of things –
We live on the edge of a sword.
Thou canst not change the many-sidedness of existence –
Our home is in a variety of countries.

See how people contradict themselves,
And how, well-meaning, they break their heads –
No longer knowing in which direction to turn,
Because they no longer see the wood for the trees.

XCVIII

If a conqueror treats the vanquished
Too harshly, he will be called a villain;
If he treats them too leniently, he will be called a traitor
In his homeland, and put on trial.
How should one act as a conqueror?
God knows. Happy the man who has no homeland.

Thou mayest succeed in a number of things –
But thou canst not make humanity reasonable.
For if man acted in the light of God,
There would be happiness – but no world history.

XCIX

If thou art in a difficult situation,
Then thou also knowest: it cannot last forever.
The faith that dwells deep within thy heart,
Breaks down unwanted walls in the soul.

Faith – or God's presence:
Liberation awaits us in our heart.

C

Man — how can he envisage the Absolute?
It is like a point, and, within ourselves, it is certitude.
As for the Infinite — it is a vast space,
And, within ourselves, it is peace, beatitude.

Truth and beauty — as Plato said:
If the True did not exist, there would be no beauty.

The Absolute radiates Infinity.

CI

Meadows and forests — our world is green;
What does this color mean?
Blue is contemplativity and yellow is joy —
Green is the world since the sun began to shine.

The same with the soul: it is made of deep contemplation
And of heart's joy — of trust in God.
Islam says: green will be our raiment in Paradise.

Heaven's meadow shines in luminous green.

CII

Encounter with the desert – the camel
Is like a mountain with majestic stride.
Why did the desert sand have to spread
Over the world, alongside the green?
Because silence too has its beauty –

The sun also blesses the empty land.
It can make fruitful, but also destroy –
Thou canst not command the heavenly heights.

Vacare Deo – says the emptiness of the sea of sand.
Everything says *Amor Dei* – to God be the glory.

CIII

Vacare Deo – O soul, grow still.
Laus Dei – all existence praises the Lord,
Because this lies in the nature of things;
We exist, because our being wishes to praise God.

CIV

If thou hast awakened from the sleep of self-love,
Thou wilt see of what stuff thou art made.
Say: *Deo gratias*. Everything is a thanksgiving,
Because everything has drunk from the Highest Good.

CV

Serenitas — therefore resignation;
And *certitudo* — therefore trust in God.
It may be that I have said this a hundred times already;
May God help me to build the bridge.

CVI

Thou readest in the Psalms
How David cried out to the Lord Most High —
How fervent and profound
Is his voice indeed!
Beautiful is God remembrance
That lies in the Supreme Name —
And beautiful are the words
With which God give us joy.

CVII

In my childhood, those around me
Would not believe that the sacred dwelt in me —
That in a child, who was so unlike them,
Something of the Highest Truth could be enthroned.
So they sought to destroy my cast of soul —
Whereas I could hear the words of God.

CVIII

Squirrels are small compared with elephants;
People say this is so for the eye of man,
But not in itself. Now, man is God's measure —
Say not that a God-willed measure does not count.

It seems to me that the elephant is big in itself;
You see that there is no bigger land animal.
The earth knows what its cargo should be;
God says: I decide what is big.

There is the relative and there is the Absolute —
But there is also a truth between the two:
The relatively absolute —
When God, like lightning, resounds within existence.

CIX

Truth and action. Man forges his own destiny.
Music and love — this is a gentler realm;
But both worlds are profoundly contained in existence —
And in God, who sees all possibilities.

CX

Absurdity bears witness to All-Possibility —
For what exists, cannot but be.
Therefore thou must have resignation and trust —
Without the one, the other would not be.

God permits, but limits, the absurd;
Therefore be trusting. Only in God
And in His Will, can the soul reap benefit.

CXI

He who wants to understand metaphysics aright
Must also have faith and obedience.
The world-wheel turns, without asking thee
Why, how, where and when — so remain still.

CXII

Besides resignation and trust
There is also dispassion — did not Solomon say
"All is vanity"? See how the noise of the world
Is shattered against the wall of a wise heart.

Vairāgya — the peace of soul of the *Vedāntī;*
Shankarāchārya's peace — *shānti, shānti.*

CXIII

Consider the church and the multitude of saints —
Admire them, but be circumspect:
The church also needed, *nolens volens,*
Plato and Aristotle, the heathens.

Religio and *sophia* — be just,
And understand that humanity lives from both.

CXIV

Truth and music. Truth bespeaks the Absolute,
Music bespeaks the Infinite —
It is a song of praise which,
From deep within the heart, ascends to the Most High.

CXV

Woman incarnates beauty, and hence love —
Her body is made for music and dance.
In music and dance, the Sacred speaks —
If God has previously awakened the spirit in her.

CXVI

They built for me a veranda,
A walkway with wall and roof by my house —
So that each day I can walk peacefully
Protected from rain and roaring wind.

It is a symbol of solitary wayfaring.
Be alone with God — and thou wilt be one with the Self
And with everything good. He whose soul
Rests in the True is embraced by the Sovereign Good.

CXVII

I always like to return to Shankara,
For he is the deep happiness of my existence;
Brahma satyam — I cannot say anything better.
May God help me to carry life's burden.

CXVIII

If we love men without loving God,
Our deepest core cannot be happy.
Earthly love cannot delight the heart
Outside the wine of God's love.

Ye ask me if God is jealous —
I answer: yes and no;
He looks with a loving gaze at the believing soul —
But idolaters are indifferent to Him.

CXIX

A Holy Scripture is not only great through its content,
It is also a sacrament: a heavenly gift,
A bread, a drink. Thou livest from its thoughts,
But also from its being — it frees thee from thy burdens
And the limitations of thy soul.

CXX

There is nothing greater in man than the Intellect;
And there is nothing greater in the Intellect than Reality —
The consciousness that radiates from the Sovereign Good,
And then rends the veil of all illusion,

And reveals Isis — naked Being,
Which says within thine inmost self: heart, thou art mine.

CXXI

There is only One God and no other —
And nothing is greater than the remembrance of God.
Thus speaks the Sufi — firstly in his mind;
And then he lives it in his inmost depths.

Truth that motionlessly rises upwards;
Holiness that strives towards depth.
The mountain; then the river that springs from it
And fades away in the ocean's infinity.

CXXII

Thou mayest love many things in this world;
But do not forget that what comes, passes away —
That in time, and under the vault of the sky,
Only what is from the Spirit is permanent.

Blessèd the man who, in the world, trusts in the Spirit.
Truth is the bride of the wise heart —
The True that is inscribed in God.

CXXIII

"This is what we have already experienced,"
So say the blessèd souls, according to the Koran,
When, after life's illusion, they enjoy
What heavenly powers prepared for the pious.

For what we love in the domain of time,
Has its roots in Eternity —
We loved, because we strove towards the Eternal.

CXXIV

If thou wishest to be happy, then seek what
Is born out of happiness as such.
He who seeks happiness in the realm of illusion
Has already lost his wishful dream.

Memento: *O beata certitudo*
In Deo — O sola beatitudo.

CXXV

Why all these didactic poems
After all that I have said in my books?
Because poetry speaks a language
That is for everyone – educated and uneducated alike –
Because it goes directly to the heart.
However, what I have to say here
Has different levels, according to Heaven's gift.

CXXVI

Grace often has a feminine form –
It is mother and bride at the same time.
Such is Mary – when she looks upon thee,
A ray from the kingdom of Heaven greets thee –
The dear Lord's saving power.

CXXVII

In the widest sense, philosophy
Is thinking of the True. But there are two levels:
Thinking on the basis of human reason;
And Light, to which the sage refers –

Divine inspiration. Plato combined the two,
And so did the Stagirite. Shankara
Contemplates the mysteries of Heaven's meadows.

CXXVIII

A thinker wrote that we do not love the good –
The good be only what we arbitrarily love.
If this is the total result of his insights,
It would have been better if the thinking had never occurred.

CXXIX

Sharp and profound discernment between
What is real and what is mere appearance;
Permanent concentration on what we recognize as true –
Blessèd the one who never forgets God's ways.

CXXX

Inwardness based on certitude:
This is the primordial law and happiness of the spirit;
And then, the soul's elevation above earthly things –
The Way that comes from God and leads back to God.

Notes

Notes to *Songs without Names IX*

1. The author says "misosophers."
2. Sanskrit: An "untouchable," from the point of view of the Hindu caste system.

Notes to *Songs without Names X*

1. Hindus and Iranians.

Notes to *Songs without Names XI*

1. "Intellect" always means "Spirit" and not "mind."
2. This may have been in 1922, when the author was fifteen.

Notes to *Songs without Names* XII

1. The author, while extolling "gnosis" (Knowledge of God), is not a proponent of "gnosticism," an early Christian heresy. Nevertheless, in this poem, he borrows from "gnosticism" the terms that describe the three fundamental human types. As regards "gnosis," it is expressed in the words of Christ: "Ye shall know the Truth, and the Truth shall make you free."

Editor's Note: A few poems do not appear in this edition, but the original order and numbering have been retained.

Index of Foreign Quotations

Aham Brahmāsmi (Sanskrit): "I am Brahma" (pp.25, 222, 223).
Adiáphora (Greek): something indifferent or non-essential. Generally used in a theological sense, for things not regarded as essential to faith and on which the Church has given no decision: for instance, things which are neither expressly commanded nor forbidden by Scripture. Used philosophically, it refers to matters that are morally neutral (p.115).
Amor Dei (Latin): "Love of God" (pp.266, 273).
Ars sine scientia nihil (Latin): "Art without knowledge is nothing" (p.39).
Audiatur et altera pars (Latin): "Let the other side also be heard" (p.46).
Benedico te (Latin): "I bless thee" (p.49).
Brahma satyam (Sanskrit): "God is real" (pp.40, 129, 212, 246, 277).
Carpe diem (Latin): "Seize the day"; Horace (p.81).
Corpus, anima, spiritus (Latin): "Body, soul, spirit" (p.118).
Corruptio optimi est pessima (Latin): "Corruption of the best is worst" (p.160).
De gustibus non est disputandum (Latin): "There is no disputing about tastes" (p.169).
Deo gratias (Latin): "Thanks be to God" (pp.75, 240, 273).
Deo juvante (Latin): "With God's help" (pp.99, 200, 201).
Deus sive natura (Latin): "God or nature" (p.266).
Dies irae, dies illa, / Solvet saeclum in favilla (Latin): "The day of wrath, that day will dissolve the world into ashes." Medieval Latin hymn, sung on All Souls' Day (author: Thomas de Celano, 13th century) (p.132).
Dieu le veut (French): "God wants it" (p.120).
Dieu premier servi (French): "God is served first" in the words of Saint Joan of Arc (p.222).
Ex Oriente Lux (Latin): "Light [comes] from the East" (p.134).
Felix culpa (Latin): "Happy fault" (p.48).
Festina lente (Latin): "Hurry slowly" (p.81).
Hagar Firdaus bar ruye zamīn ast, / Hamīn ast u-hamīn ast u-hamīn ast (Persian): "If there is a Paradise on earth, it is here, it is here, it is here" (p.221).
Homo faber (Latin): "Man the maker" (p.123).
Laus Dei (Latin): "Praise of God" (p. 273).
Mā shā'a 'Llāh (Arabic): "What God has willed" (p.51).
Memento mori (Latin): "Remember that you are mortal" (p.186).
Nolens volens (Latin): "Whether willing or not" (p.276).
Om, bhūr bhuvah svah / Tat Savitur varenyam (Sanskrit): From the Gayatri Hymn, *Yajurveda*, the full form of which is: *Om, bhūr bhuvah svah / Tat Savitur varenyam/ Bhargo Devasya dheemahi / Dheeyo yo nah prachodayaat*: "Om, earth, air, and the heavenly expanse; Let me praise that Savita (the Sun God); Let us meditate upon the glory of the Deva; May He enlighten our intellect." (pp.246, 247).
Om namah shivāya (Sanskrit): "Om, I bow to Lord Shiva" (p.201).
Om, shanti, shanti; aham Brahmāsmi (Sanskrit): "Hail, peace, peace; I am Brahma." From the *Brihadaranyaka Upanishad* (p.25).

Opportet haereses esse (Latin): "It is opportune that there be heresies" (p.48).
Pues tanto a mi Amado quiero, / que muero porque no muero (Spanish): "For I love my Beloved so much, that I am dying because I don't die" (p.17).
Quidquid agis, prudenter agas; / respice finem (Latin): "Whatever you do, do it prudently; consider the result" (p.81).
Quod licet Jovi, numquam licet bovi (Latin): "What is lawful for Jupiter, is not lawful for the ox" (p.119).
Respice finem (Latin): "Consider the result" (p.43).
Sanctificetur Nomen Tuum (Latin): "Hallowed be Thy Name" (Lord's Prayer) (p.223).
Sola beatitudo (Latin): "Sole beatitude" (p.122).
Soma, psyche, pneuma (Greek): "Body, soul, spirit" (p.118).
Vacare Deo (Latin): "To be empty in God" (pp.214, 266, 273).
Vincit omnia Veritas (Latin): "Truth conquers all" (p.121).

Index of First Lines

Books by Frithjof Schuon

The Transcendent Unity of Religions
Spiritual Perspectives and Human Facts
Gnosis: Divine Wisdom
Language of the Self
Stations of Wisdom
Understanding Islam
Light on the Ancient Worlds
In the Tracks of Buddhism
Treasures of Buddhism
Logic and Transcendence
Esoterism as Principle and as Way
Castes and Races
Sufism: Veil and Quintessence
From the Divine to the Human
Christianity/Islam: Essays on Esoteric Ecumenicism
Survey of Metaphysics and Esoterism
In the Face of the Absolute
The Feathered Sun: Plains Indians in Art and Philosophy
To Have a Center
Roots of the Human Condition
Images of Primordial and Mystic Beauty: Paintings by Frithjof Schuon
Echoes of Perennial Wisdom
The Play of Masks
The Transfiguration of Man
The Eye of the Heart
Form and Substance in the Religions

Edited Writings of Frithjof Schuon

The Essential Writings of Frithjof Schuon, ed. Seyyed Hossein Nasr
The Fullness of God: Frithjof Schuon on Christianity,
ed. James S. Cutsinger
Prayer Fashions Man: Frithjof Schuon on the Spiritual Life,
ed. James S. Cutsinger
Art from the Sacred to the Profane: East and West
ed. Catherine Schuon

Poetry by Frithjof Schuon

Sulamith, Berna, Urs Graf Verlag, 1946

Tage- und Nächtebuch, Berna, Urs Graf Verlag, 1946

The Garland, Abodes, 1994

Road to the Heart: Poems, World Wisdom Books, 1995

Liebe, Verlag Herder Freiburg im Breisgau, 1997

Leben, Verlag Herder Freiburg im Breisgau, 1997

Glück, Verlag Herder Freiburg im Breisgau, 1997

Sinn, Verlag Herder Freiburg im Breisgau, 1997

Amor y Vida. Poesías, Mallorca, José J. de Olañeta, Editor, 1999

Sinngedigchte/Poésies didactiques, Volumes 1-10,
Sottens, Suisse, Editions Les Sept Flèches, 2000-2005

Songs for a Spiritual Traveler: Selected Poems, World Wisdom, 2001

Adastra & Stella Maris: Poems by Frithjof Schuon, World Wisdom, 2003

Autumn Leaves & The Ring: Poems by Frithjof Schuon, World Wisdom, 2007

Songs without Names: Volumes I-VI, World Wisdom, 2006

Songs without Names: Volumes VII-XII, World Wisdom, 2006

World Wheel: Volumes I-III, World Wisdom, 2006

World Wheel: Volumes IV-VII, World Wisdom, 2006